The Mystery Fancier

Volume 4 Number 6
November/December 1980

The MYSTERY FANcier

Volume 4 Number 6
November/December, 1980

TABLE OF CONTENTS

```
MYSTERIOUSLY SPEAKING . . . . . . . . . . . . . . . . . . . 1
Spy Series Characters in Hardback, Part V,
     by Barry Van Tilburg. . . . . . . . . . . . . . . . . . 4
Favorite Magazine Issues: Manhunt (3:6), by Jeff Banks. . . 7
Old Time Radio Lives, by Carl Larsen. . . . . . . . . . . . 9
Pow-Wow on the Potomac (Bouchercon), by John Nieminski. . . 12
Bouchercon Scrapbook, photos by John Nieminski (mostly),
     commentary by Guy M. Townsend . . . . . . . . . . . . . 19
IT'S ABOUT CRIME, by Marvin Lachman . . . . . . . . . . . . 31
VERDICTS (More Reviews) . . . . . . . . . . . . . . . . . . 34
THE DOCUMENTS IN THE CASE (Letters) . . . . . . . . . . . . 40
```

The MYSTERY FANcier
(USPS:428-590)
is edited and published bi-monthly by Guy M. Townsend,
840 East Main Street, #5, Blytheville, Arkansas 72315.
Contributions of all descriptions are welcomed.

SUBSCRIPTION RATES: Domestic second class mail, $9.00 per year (6 issues); overseas surface mail, $9.00; overseas airmail, $12.00. Overseas subscribers please pay in international money order, check drawn on U.S. bank, or currency; no checks drawn on foreign banks, please.

Second class postage paid at Blytheville, Arkansas

Copyright 1980 by Guy M. Townsend
All rights reserved for contributors
ISSN:0146-3160

Mysteriously Speaking...

Lots of news, the principal item this time being that we are still in business. The number of positive responses topped a hundred the last week in December, so TMF will be around for at least another year. I really am pleased; from time to time it has seemed an awful albatross, but I've made quite a few friends (not to mention a few good enemies) through these pages, and I didn't relish the thought of losing contact.

Two responses in particular I would like to mention. The first one, from a subscriber-and-spouse combination, really floored me. This couple, believe it or not, actually offered to underwrite whatever loss I might take on the first two issues of volume 5, if I would just continue publication. That's a remarkable offer, considering the fact that my loss on a recent issue was around $200, and they could have been committing themselves to as much as $400. But, as I've said often before, mystery fans--and TMFers in particular--are good folks. I declined the offer with profuse thanks, my heart considerably gladdened by the knowledge that they thought so much of this little magazine.

The second response was from John Nieminski. Until the current issue, John has been keeping a rather low profile in these pages, so it is possible that some of you do not know him for the genius that he is. John is, in fact, perhaps the best and wittiest writer in mystery fandom, so the nature of his response sent cold chills through my frail body. If I was really serious about giving TMF up, he wrote, he would be interested in taking it over. Now I've been blundering along for four years now, doing my usual slipshod job at the editorial helm and not feeling that I had to make any special effort so long as I delivered the goods, and there John was suggesting that he run TMF after my departure. Clearly, such a thing was unthinkable, since I would suffer so badly in the comparisons which would inevitably follow. I had, therefore, no choice but to stick with the magazine, even if the hundred commitments had not arrived in time.

However, if John is really serious about wanting to take on another publication (he already edits a Sherlockian gem called *Baker Street Miscellanea*), I don't see why we shouldn't encourage him in his madness. Surely there is room for another mystery fanzine, and I am certain that John's editorship of such a periodical would set standards for the rest of us to aim at. So, if you folks are interested, why not let John know, either through these pages or directly at the address which you will find in the letter section below. For my part, I will happily turn over my complete mailing list to him, and I might even submit one or two of the reviews which I do in my Malcom Milquetoast incarnation but which rarely show up in these pages. Seriously, folks, mystery fandom needs a general fanzine edited by John Nieminski, so let's get him committed (so to speak) before he comes to his senses.

More news: effective with volume 5, number 1, I will no longer give monetary credit toward the next year's subscription to contributors to TMF. Henceforth, people who contribute articles will receive an extra copy of the issue in which their articles appear, but everyone else--including all reviewers and letter writers--will have to content themselves with my very sincere (but non-negotiable) thanks. I hate to do this, but it's another way that I can cut down on the cost of producing this magazine. Of course, everyone who contributed to volume 4, to which the old policy applied, has earned and is urged to accept the reduced rates as listed below. By the way, there are two exceptions to this everyone-must-pay-the-full-subscription policy, and they are Steve Lewis and Marv Lachman, whose columns are regular features (Steve's Mystery*File came too late for this issue--watch it, Steve--but with the Bouchercon items taking up so much room the extra space was a boon); they, of course, will pay nothing for their subscriptions. In the list below the amounts shown reflect a credit of $1.50 for each issue in which a contributor appeared:

Bob Adey (3) $13.50
Walter Albert (1,5) $9.00
Nancy Axelrod (6) $10.50
Jane Bakerman (1,2,5,6) $6.00
John Ballinger (1) $10.50
Jeff Banks (1,2,5,6) $6.00
Ev Bleiler (4,5,6) $6.00
Jon Breen (2,6) $9.00
Myrtis Broset (6) $10.50
Toby Brust (5) $10.50
Mike Cook (1) $10.50
Bill Crider (1,3,5,6) $6.00
Mary Jean Demarr (1) $10.50
David Doerrer (1,2,5) $7.50
Fred Dueren (3,4) $9.00
Ted Dukeshire (1,2,3) $7.50
Ben Fisher (5,6) $9.00
Frank Floyd (1,6) $9.00
Ilse Goldsmith (2) $10.50
Jim Goodrich (2,4) $9.00
Jane Gottschalk (1) $10.50
Michael Greenbaum (2) $10.50
Mary Ann Grochowski (2) $10.50
John Harwood (1) $10.50
George Kelley (1,2,3) $7.50
Betty King (1) $10.50
Joe Lansdale (2) $10.50
Karen LaPorte (3) $10.50
Carl Larsen (1,4,5,6) $6.00
Bill Loeser (1,6) $9.00
Paul PcCarthy (4) $10.50
David McGee (1) $10.50
Walker Martin (2) $10.50
Dick Moskowitz (2) $10.50
Elmore Mundell (6) $10.50
Ellen Nehr (1,4) $9.00
Mike Nevins (1-6) -0-
John Nieminski (6) $10.50
Jim O'Donnell (2,4) $12.00
Becky Reineke (5,6) $9.00
Robert Samoian (2,6) $9.00
Sandy Sandulo (1) $10.50
Howard Sharpe (1) $13.50
Charles Shibuk (5,6) $9.00
Linda Toole (3,5) $9.00
Barry Van Tilburg (2-6) $4.50
R.L. Wenstrup (5) $10.50
Martin Wooster (3) $14,625

SEND MONEY TO ME AT MY NEW ADDRESS

SURPRISE--By the time you receive this issue TMF will have a new address. "Ah, yes, Townsend's quarterly move," some of you are probably saying, but I think this one is going to be the exception. You will, therefore, need to send your renewal checks--made out to Guy M. Townsend, please--to me, c/o *Practical Horseman*, 225 S. Church St., West Chester, PA 19380. I'd explain, but I haven't the time or space right now.

Another new policy--when one of you moves without giving me your new address, the postal service tears off your address label, throws the magazine away, returns the address label to me, and demands that I pay them 25¢ in order to find out what your new address is. That's just the start. I then have to take another copy of the magazine (which, with volume five, will cost $2.00), stick it into another envelope (which costs a little less than a dime), slap on about 50¢ in postage, and mail it to you at your new address. If you add that all up it comes to about three bucks that I'm out because you forgot to tell me that you were moving. Therefore, from now on I will *not* automatically replace issues which are thrown away by the postal people (they throw them away because second class mail is not forwardable); I'll simply make the change of address on my card file and see to it that all future issues go to the new address. If you want a copy of the issue you missed, it'll cost you three bucks. Of course, this applies only to issues which are lost because of a subscriber's failure to notify me of a new address--issues which for any other reason fail to arrive will be replaced at no charge.

Another item. The Stout Bibliography on which John McAleer, Jud Sapp, Arriean Schemer and I worked for a couple of years was published by Garland in December. Entitled *Rex Stout: An Annotated Primary and Secondary Bibliography*, it is priced at an outrageous $30 per, but if any of you are fool enough to want to pay that amount for it I'll be happy to sell you a copy (autograph optional) for $30, postpaid. Yes, I get an author's discount, but I'd like to make a little money out of it. I've no idea how long it will take for me to send the book to you, since Garland is taking its sweet time sending them to me. You may prefer to buy the bood directly through your book seller. Or you may prefer to give it a pass altogether--at $30 a throw, it sure as hell isn't going to make the best-seller charts.

Speaking of books recently published, or about to be published, our own Jon Breen has one entitled *What About Murder?* which is being published (has been published?) by Scarecrow Press. Jon tells me that he mentions TMF in it, so it's bound to be a real class act. No information on cost--perhaps Jon will tell us in a letter to TMF 5:1.

One last thing, then I'll bundle this thing up and get it off to the printer. In Walter's Line-Up in the last issue he mentions a publication called *The Thorndyke File*, published by Philip Asdell. John McAleer (121 Follen Rd., Lexington, MA 02173) has advised me that he is taking over the *File* but is still short of the 120 subscribers (at $5 per year) he needs to survive. Five bucks ain't much to keep a fanzine alive, so if you've got the slightest interest at all in the good Doctor T., drop a finif in the mail to John right away.

I know there are dozens of things I should say and can't remember, but time is short and I've got to get this finished so that I can get the hell out of Arkansas.

Ta.

SPY SERIES CHARACTERS IN HARDBACK, V
By Barry Van Tilburg

DOSSIER #30: Hugh North.
CREATED BY: Francis Van Wyck Mason.
OCCUPATION: American military agent for Army Intelligence, G-2.
ASSOCIATES: No regulars.
WEAPONS: Since he is in the military, he uses all kinds.
OTHER COMMENTS: North deals with murders having anything to do with intelligence or political situations. He starts the series as a captain but soon rises to major and then colonel. The stories involve a good deal of laboratory work, and Mason keeps his character and his plots up to date. The last book, *The Deadly Orbit Mission*, takes Hugh North to Tangiers to find out why a Russian satellite armed with a hydrogen bomb is orbiting along a line of key U.S. cities.

The Vesper Service Murders (Doubleday, 1931; Eldon, 1937).
The Fort Terror Murders (Doubleday, 1931; Eldon, 1936).
The Yellow Arrow Murders (Doubleday, 1932; Eldon, 1936).
The Branded Spy Murders (Doubleday, 1932; Eldon, 1936).
The Sulu Seas Murders (Doubleday, 1933; Eldon, 1936).
The Shanghai Bund Murders (Doubleday, 1933; Eldon, 1937).
The Budapest Parade Murders (Doubleday, 1935; Eldon, 1936).
The Washington Legation Murders (Doubleday, 1935; Eldon, 1937).
The Hong Kong Airbase Murders (Doubleday, 1936).
The Seven Seas Murders (Doubleday, 1937; Eldon, 1937).
The Cairo Garter Murders (Doubleday, 1938; Jarrolds, 1938).
The Bucharest Ballerina Murders (Doubleday, 1940; Jarrolds, 1941)
The Rio Casino Intrigue (Doubleday, 1941; Jarrolds, 1942).
Saigon Singer (Doubleday, 1946; Jarrolds, 1948).
Dardanelles Derelict (Doubleday, 1949; Barker, 1950).
Himalayan Assignment (Doubleday, 1952).
Two Tickets for Tangier (Doubleday, 1955).
The Gracious Lilly Affair (Doubleday, 1957; Hale, 1958).
Secret Mission to Bangkok (Doubleday, 1960).
Trouble in Burma (Doubleday, 1962).
Zanzibar Intrigue (Doubleday, 1963; Hale, 1964).
Maracaibo Mission (Doubleday, 1965).
The Deadly Orbit Mission (Doubleday, 1968).

DOSSIER #31: Idwal Rees.
CREATED BY: Berkeley Mather.
OCCUPATION: Agent for British Intelligence.
ASSOCIATES: Sarafas, his slave; Gaffer, his boss; and Wainwright, a traitor.
WEAPONS: .38 caliber pistol.
OTHER COMMENTS: Having been born in the East, Rees has a natural knack for getting around and getting things done there. He is of mixed parentage and can pass himself off as a native of different countries. He can be very dangerous when provoked. In the last book, *With Extreme Prejudice*, Rees is out to destroy the people who are backing terrorists in the Middle East.

The Pass Beyond Kashmir (Collins, 1960; Scribners, 1960).
The Break in the Line (Collins, 1970; published as *The Break* by Scribners, 1970).

The Terminators (Collins, 1971; Scribners, 1971).
Snowline (Collins, 1973; Scribners, 1973).
With Extreme Prejudice (Collins, 1975; Scribners, 1975).

DOSSIER #32: Charles Hood
CREATED BY: James Mayo
OCCUPATION: Special troubleshooter for various departments of British Intelligence.
ASSOCIATES: The Circus.
WEAPONS: Hands and guns.
OTHER COMMENTS: The Circus, for which Hood works, is an International financial combine (oil, chemicals, industrials, banking, art dealing, shipping, financing, underwriting, and diamonds) whose interests often parallel the government's. Hood is very often very violent. In *The Man Above Suspicion* he finds a traitor in high places. Vince Edwards played Hood in the movie version of *Hammerhead*.
Hammerhead (Heinemann, 1964; Morrow, 1964).
Let Sleeping Girls Lie (Heinemann, 1965; Morrow, 1965).
Shamelady (Heinemann, 1966; Morrow, 1966).
Once in a Lifetime (Heinemann, 1968; published as *Sergeant Death* by Morrow, 1968).
The Man Above Suspicion (Heinemann, 1969).
Asking for It (Heinemann, 1971).

DOSSIER #33: Harrigan and Hoeffler.
CREATED BY: Patrick O'Malley.
OCCUPATION: Agents for a special secret branch of American intelligence dealing with counterspies.
ASSOCIATES: Their boss, who they call "The Chief."
WEAPONS: Both can use guns, but one is an electronics genius who comes up with all kinds of gadgetry. In *The Affair of John Donne* one uses a rifle while the other uses a rope to lasso the bad guys.
OTHER COMMENTS: Harrigan and Hoeffler seem too knowledgeable to be real; O'Malley was either a genius himself or was a very good researcher. He also had a very good sense of humor. In *The Affair of the Bumbling Briton*, the Briton in question is a James Bondish agent who happens to get himself kidnapped while on a train. (James Bond buffs are familiar with Bond's habit of getting into battles on trains.) Harrigan and Hoeffler are sent to find Britain's master agent before he gets himself killed.
The Affair of the Red Mosaic (Mill Morrow, 1961).
The Affair of Swan Lake (Mill Morrow, 1962).
The Affair of Jolie Madame (Mill Morrow, 1963).
The Affair of Chief Strongheart (Mill Morrow, 1964).
The Affair of John Donne (Mill Morrow, 1964).
The Affair of the Bumbling Briton (Mill Morrow, 1965).
The Affair of the Blue Pig (Mill Morrow, 1965).

DOSSIER #34: Philis.
CREATED BY: Ritchie Perry.
OCCUPATION: Agent for British espionage organization [SR(2)].
ASSOCIATES: Works alone, but sarcastically enjoys the company of his boss, Pawson.
WEAPONS: Pistols, mostly.
OTHER COMMENTS: Philis did a lot of odd jobs before he became a spy. His last was a kind of black market, import-export

business (see *The Fall Guy*). The books are very violent.
The Fall Guy (Houghton, 1972; Collins, 1972).
A Hard Man to Kill (Houghton, 1973; published as *Nowhere man* by Collins, 1973).
Ticket to Ride (Collins, 1973; Houghton, 1974).
Holiday With a Vengeance (Collins, 1974; Houghton, 1975).
Your Money and Your Wife (Collins, 1975; Houghton, 1976).
One Good Death Deserves Another (Collins, 1976; Houghton, 1977).
Dead End (Collins, 1977).
Dutch Courage (Collins, 1978).
Bishop's Pawn (Collins, 1979).
Grand Slam (Collins, 1980).

DOSSIER #35: Andy and Arabella Blake.
CREATED BY: Richard Powell.
OCCUPATION: Agents for Army Intelligence.
ASSOCIATES: None named.
WEAPONS: Andy hates guns, but Arabella is quite handy with anything.
OTHER COMMENTS: Arabella, or Arab, as Andy calls her, is the stronger of the two. She usually starts their adventures and then cons Andy into carrying on with her plans. Before and after the war they run an antique shop.
Don't Catch Me (Simon & Schuster, 1943).
All Over But the Shooting (Simon & Schuster, 1944).
Lay That Pistol Down (Simon & Schuster, 1945).
Shoot If You Must (Simon & Schuster, 1946).
And Hope to Die (Simon & Schuster, 1947).

DOSSIER #36: David Audley and Colonel Butler.
CREATED BY: Anthony Price.
OCCUPATION: Agents for British Army Intelligence.
ASSOCIATES: Audley's wife, Faith.
WEAPONS: Audley prefers to use his brains; Butler, the soldier, can use any weapon available.
OTHER COMMENTS: Before entering the intelligence game, Audley was a teacher of history, and history leads him into many of his exploits. In *Our Man in Camelot* the legendary city and treasure of King Arthur are the basis for the plot.
The Labyrinth Makers (Gollancz, 1970; Doubleday, 1971).
The Alamut Ambush (Gollancz, 1971; Doubleday, 1972.
Colonel Butler's Wolf (Gollancz, 1972; Doubleday, 1973).
October Men (Gollancz, 1973; Doubleday, 1974).
Other Paths to Glory (Gollancz, 1974; Doubleday, 1975).
Our Man in Camelot (Gollanzc, 1975; Doubleday, 1976).
War Game (Gollancz, 1976; Doubleday, 1977).
The '44 Vintage (Gollancz, 1978; Doubleday, 1978).
Tomorrow's Ghost (Gollancz, 1979).
Hour of the Donkey (Gollancz, 1980).

FAVORITE MAGAZINE ISSUES:
Manhunt (3:6), June 1955

By R. Jeff Banks

    The prime reason this is my favorite, rather than any one of the four 1953 issues which serialized Mickey Spillane's longest known magazine story "Somebody's Watching Me", is that this issue reprinted the novel complete, adding a 48-page bonus to the magazine's size, thus making it the fattest issue up to that time. There is a good chance it contained more fiction wordage than any other issue at all, but my *Manhunt* collection is spotty (and right now scattered too) enough that I can't be certain. More on the novel later.

    Let's open my favorite magazine. It consists of 192 pages, not counting covers, and only carries a single, half-page ad inside. This last detail not only means it is chockful of good reading, but is also probably indicative of a major reason for the magazine's failure a decade later. Back covers, inside and out, are an ad for Detective Book Club; even if the prices make me drool, I wouldn't clip that coupon. Front cover is a very fine "frightened girl", unfortunately with no artist's signature nor credit. Inside cover is a contents page listing seven features (a legal puzzle, a detective puzzle contest, announcement of correct solution and winner of a previous contest, three true crime articles, and a full page of capsule biographies on five of the authors included) and ten pieces of fiction.

    The fiction leads off with "The Reluctant Client", a fine Mike Shayne short. Remember that these were the days when Davis Dresser *was* writing magazine fiction signed Brett Halliday, and remember, too, that Dresser was a master of the shorter forms. The only "regulars" in the story are Shayne, his secretary Lucy and his *bete noir* Peter Painter, but Dresser has room to show the three clearly and to describe a murdre and solution. The illustration by Dirk (or Dick) Shelton catches the spirit of the story beautifully. The second short is "Interrogation" by Jack Ritchie, a telling attack on police brutality. James Sentz visualized the "third degree" session in a sketch full of highly effective distortions. George Bagby's very short "Body Snatcher" comes next. It includes development of an interesting protagonist, murder, and a surprise ending. I've always preferred Bagby's short fiction to his novels. Shelton's illustration is good, but not as effective as the one for the Shayne story.

    "Code 197" by Richard Prather, who always wrote his own short fiction, which is a guarantee of enjoyment to those many fans who enjoy his book-length work, features Shell Scott with the usual trappings. Tom O'Sullivan illustrates this story well, and it is the first of two short novelets included. The other, "The Makeshift Martini" by Jack Webb, is near the end of the book. This one features Webb's Airport Detail, a series that was pretty short and ran exclusively (I think) in *Manhunt*. I used to read the Airport Detail stories, but never bought an issue just to get one, and I only bought occasional issues of the magazine anyway back in those "good old days" when they could be had for the cover price. This is another

7

way of saying that the series was not Webb's best effort, but this (as I recall) is an above-average entry. Sentz's illustration captures one of its most dramatic moments.

The next short story, "Decoy" by Hal Ellson, also has a well chosen and executed illo, but the artist's signature is illegible. The story is the old, old one of "thieves fall out", but enlivened by the telling of it in present tense as well as first person. Radio fans will remember this was also the tense effectively employed for the hero's "voice over" narration in Spillane's Mike Hammer show scripts. It is surprising to me that it was used so sparingly in printed fiction. The remaining shorts are both banished to the back of the book. "The Dead Grin" (illustrated by "Lee") is a Johnny Liddell short story by Frank Kane. This writer never achieved the status to justify having a "ghost", but he often wrote magazine fiction to "shill" for his quite competent novels. Johnny investigates a fraudulent insurance claim in this story, but the transparent mistake of the widow masks a real surprise ending. "The Vicious Young" by Pat Stradley is the shortest fiction in this issue, but it manages to catch the atmosphere of woman-in-danger nicely. Illustration is by Sentz again.

"The Careful Man" by Max Franklin (with a single, full-page and very good illustration by O'Sullivan) is the first of two "novels". Its 43 pages and 15 chapters may contain as many as 30,000 words, certainly no more. It is the first person story of an insurance murderer ("bluebeard") concentrating on his last two killings, which I suppose is predictable enough. When I first read it, at age twenty, the surprise ending of his career was plenty surprising for me, but when I reread it for this review I discovered a way (I think) to improve on it. That I'll probably try as a summer writing project--quite literally, though, that's a different story.

The *piece-de-resistance* is the Spillane novel. It runs 45,000 or more words, spanning 25 chapters (unusual for Spillane, who usually writes about half as many chapters in a 60,000-word book). Only the first three pix are signed--and, again, in a scribble--but they're probably all by the same more-than-competent illustrator. It is also worthy of note that about seven years later *Manhunt* again reprinted the complete novel, and darn few magazines published even any piece of short fiction on three separate occasions. It was retitled "I Come to Kill You" in its final appearance.

Unlike the situation of the Mick's usual book-length fiction (but sometimes to be seen in his books of novelets such as *Tough Guys* and *Killer Mine*), the hero is (at least at the outset) a rather un-Macho victim. Spillane fans will be aware that even Hammer was short on macho at the beginning of *The Girl Hunters*, perhaps his most memorable appearance.

OLD TIME RADIO LIVES

LOOK FOR IT IN THE MORNING EXPRESS!

By Carl Larsen

Ever so often, while traveling through an unfamiliar neighborhood, I will pass a bar named the Blue Note. Invariably, I am tempted to go in and order a beer. If I yield to that temptation, I find that almost invariably the beer comes in a bottle. But never have I found what I'm really looking for; a slightly disreputable newspaper photographer and his faithful female companion. And the bartender is never, never named Ethelbert.

If you found the above to be at all coherent, you must be old enough to remember names like Sportsman's Park, Ebbets Field and Wendy Warren. If it all read like an aging dipsomaniac's reverie, permit me to explain my attraction to watering holes of that particular shade. The Blue Note Café was the office-away-from-the-office of Flashgun Casey, ace photographer of *The Morning Express*. Aiding him in covering the crime news of a great city was ace reporter Anne Williams. She also abetted him at the Blue Note where Ethelbert, the head bartender, dispensed firewater and philosophy, both to the background music provided by the pianist whose mood gave the lounge its name.

Although George Harmon Coxe had created Casey for *Black Mask*, he apparently had little if anything to do with the radio show, not even getting a nod in the credits. *Flashgun Casey* came to radio in 1943. Soon becoming *Casey, Crime Photographer*, its final title was simply *Crime Photographer*. The show was on continuously until 1950, returning for a last hurrah from 1953 to 1955. Alonzo Deen Cole, who had gained fame for the pioneer horror show, *The Witch's Tale*, wrote many of the scripts. Staats Cotsworth (what a great name! what a great voice!) was Casey for the whole run. Long-suffering Anne Williams was portrayed by Lesley Woods, Betty Furness and Jan Miner, among others. Long-serving Ethelbert was John Gibson. Casey's friendly antagonist Captain Logan was first played by Jackson Beck and then by Bernard Lenrow. Heard in supporting roles was Art Carney. Tony Marvin, paradigm of a CBS staff announcer, sold ANCHOR HOCKING (his stentorian tones seemingly capitalized the brand name). Marvin was also long-suffering as Arthur Godfrey's straight-man. In 1948 a change of sponsors led to Bill Cullen asking, "Which twin has the Toni?" Another of the little Godfreys, Archie Bleyer, was music director. The Blue Note piano was caressed first by Herman Chittison and then by Teddy Wilson. Wilson, of course, is a legend among jazzophiles; Chittison is a legend among jazz pianists.

"The Queen of the Amazons," a sample issue from what some consider Casey's best years (1946-1950), was first broadcast on January 8, 1948. The Blue Note was Casey's frame; the show opened and closed there. The Amazon caper opens with a very cold Casey charging in and demanding a "warmer-upper." Ethelbert obliges, observing, "I guess winter's pretty hard on you delicate people." "Nuts to you," cleverly rejoins Casey.

Anne Williams arrives to interrupt the battle of wits. does she want coffee? No can do: the heartless city desk has come up with another assignment. An attempted burglary has been thwarted near the Lindenhurst Aircraft Plant. And by a woman! The two "yeggs" are in cells at the old turnpike police station. Casey complains about the forty-mile drive in zero weather. Anne explains that they will be playing up the comedy angle because the "little farmerette" who stopped the crime was formerly a circus strong woman whose speciality had been bending iron bars into pretzel shapes.

This is not amusing enough to quiet Casey's grousing: he's cold! Anne tells him to stop crabbing: she's cold too! (This was, after all, the era of unheated cars.) A touch of gallantry emerges when Casey adjusts her blanket and suggests that she should have stood in bed. Anne insists, "I'm no softie." Casey returns to his griping: the strong lady sounds like "a homely mass of muscle with the personality of a male gorilla."

He's wrong, of course. Although they estimate her at 6' 2" and 300 pounds, none of it fat, Millicent Hodges, aka Marinna, the Queen of the Amazons, has a pretty face, "kind of a baby face." She's also friendly and folksy: "Come inside. I like cold bracing days like this but they must be kinda tough on you little people." Anne mistakenly thinks that this offhanded jab will hold Casey for a while. Miss Hodges has been knitting socks (argyles!) for a gentleman friend, a fact which melts the mighty Casey's heart. After she primps for the photos, he assures her that she looks swell. "He's one of them flatterin' men, ain't he, Miss Williams?" observes the Amazon. Anne can only say, "Well, I've never noticed it."

They learn that, during the burglary attempt, Millicent was spending her daily hour in the cow barn. Returning to the house unexpectedly, she found the miscreants meddling with her old circus trunk. Enraged, she then taught them a good lesson. Casey pricks up his ears when she tells him that her good ole watchdog has recently been poisoned. He also observes the silver breakfast set and solid gold clock out in plain view.

Miss Hodges' gentleman friend, Ambrose Higginbotham of Lindenhurst Aircraft, stops by. His absolute refusal to pose for photos and the quick shuffle he gives to the two reporters are in sharp contrast to his Milquetoast voice.

A stop at the old turnpike police station establishes that the two yeggs in custody are an experienced safecracker and an espionage agent, that Higginbotham's credentials are impeccable and that Millicent Hodges is weak in the head where men are concerned. Casey determines to return to the farm--alone. As he explains to Anne, "Miss Hodges is a gal. When a guy wants to make himself popular in Florida, he doesn't go there with a crate of California oranges."

After a break for a commercial spiel, circus music announces Casey's return to the strong lady's lair. To make himself popular, he has brought a box of chocolate creams. He succeeds, finding out that "My friends call me Queenie," in a beautifyl scene with Millicent (Hope Emerson). Swell guy that he is, he can't keep up the con and he puts his cards face up. Queenie confesses that she's a sap for folks who lay their cards on the table. Having reached this understanding, they hurry into the bedroom to rip open the lid of the trunk. The real bad guys appear, complications ensue, and before the denouement we are treated to such lines as the criminal mastermind's, "There will be nothing personal in their punishment," and Casey's, "Until now, fella, I thought a worm was the lowest thing on earth." Before the good guys win in the end, both Casey and Queenie are slugged and tied up in her garage.

Another break, during which Tony Marvin lauds the ease of the "new soluble coffee in glass"--as easy as pouring a cup of hot water. Then we are back in the Blue Note Café. Casey is exultant; not only are the bad guys under lock and key, but he is scheduled for Queenie's next pair of argyles! Ethelbert warns Miss Williams of the impending romantic competition, quoting his sister Edna's maxim, "In wintertime the way to a man's heart begins with a pair of warm feet." Anne is silent. Perhaps, after all, it was not Casey's feet that she had hoped to warm.

Casey belonged to the relatively small category of radio mystery programs whose main characters were not detectives, either private or police. There are many Casey shows extant and deservedly so, for its combination of action, comedy and, almost, romance puts it well above the level of the average radio mystery. And Casey himself was a more fully developed character than most radio heroes. Fact and fiction abound with newspapermen in shabby raincoats who seek truth and justice through the big story. What the found often made them cynical and addicted to alcohol. Casey liked a drink and Casey had a cynical side, but he never lost his faith in an individual's power to change destiny, never stopped believing that the good guys would finally win in the end.

Casey also had a private life. His relationship with Anne Williams is the most obvious example of this. In one of the Christmas shows her voice perks up when Casey mentions his plans to get her a ring. When he qualifies it as a birthstone ring, her disappointment is painfully evident. She was, of course, doomed to single bliss owing to rule #1 governing the romantic relationships of continuing series characters, i.e., that matrimony spells an end to adventure. Marry the man off and he's as dull as dishwater.

The cocktail lounge setting provided an element of reality as well as providing a frame for the action. The Blue Note brackets also served to underscore the emotionally satisfying fact that a crime has been solved and a criminal brought to justice. The tear in the social fabric has been mended and stability regained. Shakespeare did much the same in his great plays, e.g., *Hamlet* and *Macbeth*, when, after the criminal elements in control have been dethroned, he gave the closing lines to the rightful ruler as confirmation of the restoration of order. This emotional satisfaction is apparently inherent in the mystery as genre and no doubt accounts for much of its popularity. In *Casey, Crime Photographer*, we can clearly see how crime interrupts the status quo, and how, with the solution, harmony is restored to the Blue Note.

Casey is gone now, gone the way of the flashgun, the extra edition and the nickel beer. Gone too are Staats Cotsworth and much of the audience who could appreciate adult, literate drama and melodrama. Gone are the newsboys on the corner, crippled or otherwise, and gone too seems to be any chance of not ending this essay on a blue note.

POW-WOW ON THE POTOMAC
A Report on Bouchercon XI
By John Nieminski

The first "Anthony Boucher Memorial Mystery and Detection Literature Convention" (as it is currently styled) was held in Santa Monica, California, on Memorial Day weekend back in 1970 under the sponsorship of Bruce Pelz and Charles Crayne, two science fiction fans who organized the affair as a tribute to the memory of crime fiction's premier critic-reviewer. Whether any of the eighty or so people who showed up for that initial gathering saw much of a future for the event is not a matter of record, but the organizers must be pleased indeed with the result. Their seedling root took firm hold and the Bouchercon has flourished, blooming annually for over a decade now, and sprouting up in locales as far removed from its West Coast birthplace as Boston, Chicago and New York. Get-togethers of this sort are common fare in the science fiction field, where conventions of one kind or another abound, but the yearly Bouchercon is the mystery genre's only organized gathering open to all comers and as such is eagerly anticipated by hardcore aficionados who find enjoyment in congregating periodically in a structured setting to indulge in serious and sometimes not-so-serious discussion of their favorite form of entertainment with others of like persuasion.

The latest incarnation of this moveable feast for mystery fans came off as scheduled on Columbus Day weekend in Washington, D.C., "Where [as the printed program slyly reminded the attendees] Crime Is Your Government's Business". The mantle of stewardship on this occasion fell on the shoulders of two Washington area-based Sherlockians of some note, who offered to tackle the chore after experiencing the delights of the New York Installment in 1977: Peter E. Blau, a geologist and journalist and Washington correspondent for the Petroleum Information Corporation of Denver, and Jon L. Lellenberg, a strategic analyst with a national security research organization. Sponsoring a convention like this is strictly a labor of love and the trick is to marshall sufficient help along the way to keep from losing your shirt. Ably assisted by a select cadre of locals who volunteered their services in handling related arrangements, and by cooperative folks in the media, the pair produced a varied program which blended nicely both traditional fare and offerings unique to the conference setting. If attendance is any measure of success, the total effort paid off: some 280 interested parties, from points as far away as California, showed up, making it the third largest of the eleven Bouchercons held to date.

This year's session took place on the premises of the National Press Club, a block or so removed from the two hotels at which most of the out-of-towners put up for the three day event. Despite the fears of some regulars that this departure from past practice might adversely impace on the special sort of ambience which attends a single site gathering, the decision to take advantage of the Club's facilities proved sound. The conference room was large and airy and offered a welcome amount of elbow room; bar and dining rooms were conveniently accessible on the same floor, and several good restaurants were in strolling distance also; and the walk to and from the Club seemed short indeed after the initial jaunt. If anyone was incommoded by the arrangement, it was likely those repeaters who have come to expect leisurely managed programs with late starting times. Several of these types were seen to scramble now and again to keep up with the generally timely flow of events which prevailed throughout.

Registration began promptly at the stroke of five on Friday the 10th and blended in smoothly with the traditional get-acquainted party which spread itself out in the conference area and spilled over into the adjacent cash bars. For old timers the swarming ritual is especially pleasurable, offering as it does the opportunity to greet old friends first encountered at earlier gatherings and not seen often enough in other environments. A number of the early arrivals dined on the premises and had no difficulty making their way back to the conference room for the opening ceremonies which began shortly after 8:00. Blau welcomed the registrants and covered conference arrangements with dispatch, and Lellenberg spoke briefly about local attractions and the content of the program to come, after which guest-of-honor Greg Mcdonald (author of the "Fletch" books, among other works) offered up a few remarks of welcome of his own.

The main event of the evening, a session entitled "The Movies: What Happened to My Book?", was moderated in sprightly fashion by Chris Steinbrunner, who drew out both informative and amusing anecdotes from panelists Brian Garfield, James Grady and Michael Hardwick, all of whom have been involved in one way or another with cinematic adaptations of genre novels or vice versa. The exchange focussed mainly on the differing needs of each medium, with more than passing mention made of some of the idiocies that prevail in the transition process. Garfield spoke at some length on the production background of his new film *Hopscotch*, revealing how and why a work based on a rather straightforward novel emerged as a scrcne comedy; Grady strove mightily to account for the transformation of his *Six Days of the Condor* into the snappier *Three Days* of the movie version; and Hardwick drew laughs also with a resume of the problems he faced in attempting to novelize Billy Wilder's *The Private Life of Sherlock Holmes* in two weeks without benefit of script, and his struggle to meet a two-day deadline for later revisions dictated by changes in the film. The consensus seemed to be that no good book is ever truly ruined by a bad movie version if one remembers that the book itself remains unsullied. The session led smoothly into the closing item on the program, a screening of the 1935 Warner Brothers film *G-Men*, with James Cagney dashing around in a D.C. setting reminding the audience of its immediate surroundings.

With the Bouchercon now firmly locked into a geographical rotation schedule, not too many followers are able to make it to every renewal. One who has is Anthony Boucher's widow, Phyllis White, who started off the proceedings on Saturday morning with a few opening remarks, recounting once again for the benefit of newcomers to the event how and why her late husband (christened William Anthony Parker White) chose the Boucher name as his pseudonym. The motivation was understandable enough: the existence in the writing profession of a superfluity of predecessor William Whites, a situation not calculated to ease the chore of one out to make a name for himself. The Boucher cognomen was taken from a relative on the maternal side of the family.

"Breaking Into Print" was the subject of the first of several panel discussions on the day's schedule, and featured authors Patricia Gafney, Sheila Martin and Joel Swerdlow, and St. Martin's Press editor Hope Delon in an exchange of views moderated by editor/anthologist Michele Slung. Swerdlow has one published thriller to his credit, acceptance of which was facilitated by his work as a freelance writer specializing in nonfiction crime, but Gafney and Martin have yet to see their initial efforts in print, and all three briefly related their experiences in dealing as novices with publishing houses. Delon and Slung tended to dominate the conversation somewhat, and seemed to be convinced (even if their struggling author panelists were not) that the mystery market is alive and well.

In the first of several offerings which drew on the Washington bureaucracy for inspiration and speakers, the next session--"Support Your Local FBI"--explored the role of that organization in law enforcement. It began inauspiciously with a canned sort of set-piece by Agent Sean McWeeney summarizing the dimensions of organized crime and the Bureau's approach to attacking the problem, but it livened up considerably once fellow agent Jack French took the podium and with McWeeney's help fielded a number of questions from the audience, some of which reflected perceptions of shortcomings in the agency's methods and practices. Among the topics touched on were sting operations (including the recent ABSCAM exercises), the structure and influence of the Mafia, and the highly organized criminous activities of motorcycle gangs. Not originally scheduled to appear, but added at the last minute, was former bank-robber-turned-writer Al Nussbaum, no stranger to Bouchercons, who offered his own not entirely favorable assessment of the Bureau's effectiveness along with insights into the working of the criminal mind. It was amusing indeed before the session began to behold the two agents huddled in earnest conversation with Nussbaum, once on the FBI's Ten Most Wanted List.

All of six writers comprised the ensuing panel, including Warren Adler, Carolyn Banks, Rob MacLeish, Patricia McGerr, Barbara Mertz (aka "Barbara Michaels" and "Elizabeth Peters") and Daoma Winston, and the challenging chore of orchestrating their input on the subject of "Washington in Mystery and Suspense" fell to moderator Marv Lachman, whose expertise in regionalism in the field logically dictated the assignment. And am admirable choice he proved to be, drawing out with carefully prepared and thought-provoking questions the views of the panelists on the opportunities offered by the D.C. environment as a setting for fictional crime and intrigue. There seemed to be general agreement that politically oriented novels have probably been overdone in recent years, with some books veering too much in the direction of over-sensationalism, but that the sub-genre will offer readers a hundred years from now valuable insights into the attitudes and values of our time not reflected in other contemporary records of a more traditional sort. The scheduled hour for discussion passed all too quickly, without much opportunity for audience participation, and provided considerable grist for the ensuing luncheon post mortem.

The gathering reconvened at close to the appointed hour of

1:45 with a segment entitled "Spy Versus Spy" moderated by Jon Lellenberg, in which the two speakers--John J. Gaskill, Jr., special agent involved in FBI intelligence operations, and Walter Pforzheimer, retired CIA agent--discussed the activities of their respective organizations. Gaskill seemed disinclined to go into much substantive detail, but Pforzheimer provided some interesting insights into the covert world of intelligence gathering, contrasting with examples the dull routine of the average undercover assignment in real life with the romanticized image portrayed in the James Bond kind of extravaganza. Both did extremely well, however, in making vivid the personal hazards of the profession, and each responded thoughtfully to questions which raised related moral and ethical issues.

If the realities of intelligence work established a reflective mood in the audience, it soon dissipated thanks to the ensuing session, a lively and argumentative affair which found Otto Penzler, Michael Seidman and Art Scott holding forth on the subject of "The Care and Feeding of Mystery Fans". The moderator, academician Pearl Aldrich, seemed somewhat at a loss for an opening gambit and pretty much allowed the speakers to take off in any direction they saw fit. Seidman, an editor at Charter Books and Al Hubin's announced successor at the helm of *The Armchair Detective*, used his allotted time and more to ventilate about publishing trends as seen from his perspective, forecasting hard times for the mystery genre in the face of adverse economic conditions and the corporate mentality prevalent at executive levels in the publishing industry. Penzler took somewhat the opposite stance, arguing that the field is flourishing and citing as evidence not only the success of specialized bookstores like his own, but also the appearance on the best seller lists in recent years of works by established mystery and suspense authors, the emergence on the scene of a spate of talented new writers, and the proliferation lately of books and magazines about the genre. Speaking as a self-styled "hard core" fan and collector, Scott suggested that the corpus of the literature is sufficient to satisfy all but the most gargantuan of appetites and that the average reader will likely be unperturbed by fluctuations in the market. Even the pessimists in the audience seemed cheered when near the end of the session a young lady rose in the audience to announce that her firm, Ballantine Books, was expanding its mystery line and would prospective story sellers please line up for an interview.

At this point in the proceedings an unscheduled short break was inserted, an action which served to siphon off a small portion of the audience from the remainder of the afternoon's program. Those few who saw fit to pass up the final session missed a fascinating hour covering the famous undercover sting operation of a few years back directed by D.C. police against East Coast fencing rings which led to the arrest and conviction of over 500 career criminals (and a few crooked cops and one bent district attorney) and the recovery of over $5,000,000 in stolen property. The speaker was retired D.C. Metropolitan Police Department Detective Lieutenant Robert D. Arscott, who masterminded the affair and was able to speak authoritatively about its planning and execution. The presentation began in chilling fashion with the playing of a tape recording of an incident which occurred earlier during a similar operation in New York on which was captured the sounds attending the killing of an undercover police agent by a gang of holdup men and an ensuing gun battle with police in which the criminals lost their lives. With that lead-in, Arscott had no difficulty at all in holding his listeners' attention. As he described the D.C. exercise his account became progressively hilarious with each of the numerous examples he gave of the gullibility of the victims of the sting. If audience reaction expressed both in rapt attention and by a multitude of end of session questions is any measure, Arscott's lively segment was the clear favorite among the day's events.

Those who made it back from dinner in time for the opening item on Saturday evening were treated to a performance of *The Painful Predicament of Sherlock Holmes*, a charming bit of Holmesian fluff written as a curtain raiser back in 1905 by the noted American stage actor and Sherlockian impersonator William Gillette. It runs about twenty minutes or so and is completely dominated by a would-be female client who chatters incessantly throughout, leaving Holmes with neither the opportunity nor the inclination to respond. Despite its age the piece holds up well, especially when carried off, as it was on this occasion, with verve and a sense of the ridiculous. The audience seemed to like the novelty of it and responded warmly to the efforts of the cast, which included local thespians Al Milikan, Robert Verry, Judy Simmons, and Denys Myers, assisted by FBIer Jack French.

The evening's main order of business, a session devoted to "The Reporter As Detective", began promptly at 8:30, with William Reuhlmann, author of *Saint with a Gun*, a study of fictional private eyes, at the moderator's microphone. As if to prove that no Bouchercon is complete without a glitch or two, one of the scheduled speakers--*The Brethren* co-author Scott Armstrong--failed to appear, later admitting rather shamefacedly that he simply forgot the commitment. But James Grady and Greg Mcdonald more than compensated for his absence with a long and far-ranging exploration of the topic which drew heavily on their own journalistic backgrounds, ably kept on course by an obviously well-prepared Ruehlmann. Both described how they made use of their knowledge of the workings of the newspaper world in their fiction and each in turn managed to give his listeners a feeling for the difficulties encountered by investigative reporters, both in the field and back at the office. And along the way each sprinkled the discussion with some provocative observations about the current political climate and the influence of the news media in shaping public opinion. The evening ended with a showing of *Call Northside 777*, with James Stewart starring in one of Hollywood's more successful attempts to portray realistically the reporter as sleuth.

Attendance was down slightly at Sunday morning's opening segment, despite a starting time delayed slightly to allow for the tardy arrival of those registrants who saw fit to do the Washington version of doing the town the night before. The topic was "Edgar Allan Poe: Where It All Began", and featured a duo of Poe specialists who held the stage for about an hour. Much the better of the two was Jack Sullivan, a professor of English literature at New York University and author of a recent study of the English ghost story, who summarized effectively Poe's stature and influence in the field of the macabre and his contribution to the development of the mystery story.

William Ryan, a freelance journalist and local literary scholar, followed with a rambling discourse on the circumstances surrounding Poe's death in nearby Baltimore 131 years before, offering up in the process the fruits of his own researches into the event. The subject is a perenially fascinating one, but Ryan's recitation seemed overly long on facts and short on conclusions, and was noticeably marred by a droning delivery and poor microphone technique.

The recently observed fiftieth anniversary of the death of Sir Arthur Conan Doyle brought with it some significant changes in the status of the copyrights assigned to that author's works. How these changes differ in England and the United States and how they might affect the Holmes Canon and image were the subjects of Peter Blau's introduction to the next session, which saw Michael Hardwick returning to the podium to discuss "Sherlock Holmes: The Next Fifty Years". As a traditionalist, Hardwick is apprehensive about the possible directions in which the Holmes character might be taken by modern day pasticheurs once the Canon enters fully into the public domain. He passed judgement on several of the Holmes novels of the past few years, suggesting that those which kept the standard image unsullied and retained the 19th century setting were clearly the more successful, and described in some detail how he handled the matter in his own recent effort, *Prisoner of the Devil*. His easy manner and low key wit seemed to sit well with the audience and held the interest of even those benighted few who argue that the world has had enough, no matter by whom, of Doyle's creation.

Needing no real introduction for his third appearance on the program, but getting a nicely done send-off by Jon Lellenberg anyway, Greg Mcdonald returned to the stage also for his guest-of-honor remarks, the final major event of the day. With a bow in the direction of the convention's namesake, and with some entertaining detours along the way (like a recap of his near arrest during the festivities, for eating an ice cream cone on Washington's "no food allowed" subway), he chose as his main topic the subject of criticism in the arts, including the mystery fiction field. As former arts and humanities editor with the *Boston Globe*, with the opportunity to assess the current state of the profession, he sees much being produced that lacks objectivity and feels that commentators these days tend to over-personalize their reactions, thereby inhibiting rather than encouraging effort and experimentation. Drawing on some horrible examples directed at his own work, he argued persuasively for constructive criticism flowing logically from well-defined standards, and more than made his case with the help of his own appealing brand of stylish wit.

With a roll call round of applause for those who contributed their services and talents to the affair (including Betty Cocran and John Linton who joined forces to produce the attractive program booklet) and with a few remarks from Mary Ann Grochowski, who will serve as chairman for the 1981 renewal in Milwaukee, the convention ended at almost exactly the scheduled hour of 12:30 p.m.

If comparisons must be made, this year's gathering was among the most enjoyable and entertaining of those held to date, thanks largely to the nicely varied program, obviously planned with care and carried off with scarcely a hitch and with some demonstrated concern for the comfort and convenience of registrants. The atmosphere was relaxed throughout, and plenty of opportunities were available to participate freely in those side activities which repeat attendees find so attractive: poring through the wares of book dealers in the huckster room between sessions; converting strangers into acquaintances and acquaintances into friends; gossiping until all hours in one room party or another; and trading contact with the rest of the world for a couple of days of innocent and relaxing self indulgence. As Hercule Poirot once said about something entirely different, "It is completely unimportant. That is why it is so interesting."

About the Author

John Nieminski is an eighty-nine-year-old mystery buff living in a nursing home on the outskirts of Chicago where he entertains morbid curiosity seekers with anecdotes about Anna Katherine Green, with whom he once engaged in a liaison. An ex-boulevardier, he now abhors the bustle of the city and prefers to while away his time puttering with his collection of the complete works of "Ellery Queen", in which he has uncovered a secret cipher which reveals the author's true identity. He is presently engaged in writing a novel, a poem, a short story, a broadside and a beer coaster, all of which reflect the influence of Erle Stanley Gardner's literary style. Soon to be published is his long-awaited index to *The Mysterious Times*, said to be his *chef-d'oeuvre*.

BOUCHERCON SCRAPBOOK

After the humiliating experience of taking some remarkably pedestrian photographs at the Chicago Bouchercon and then reproducing them as indistinguishable smudges in these pages a few years back, I went to Washington armed with the firm determination to take *good* photographs, which captured the true spirit of Bouchercon, and then print them in sparkling clear detail in TMF. All went according to plan until I tried to take my first picture and my damned electronic flash wouldn't discharge. In desperation, I decided to shoot my ASA 400 film as though it were rated 1600 and pray that the darkroom worker at the newspaper could do something with it. Unfortunately, that didn't work out well at all; however, John Nieminski was taking photos too, with a flash that *did* work, and he has allowed me to use some of his shots in place of my own. 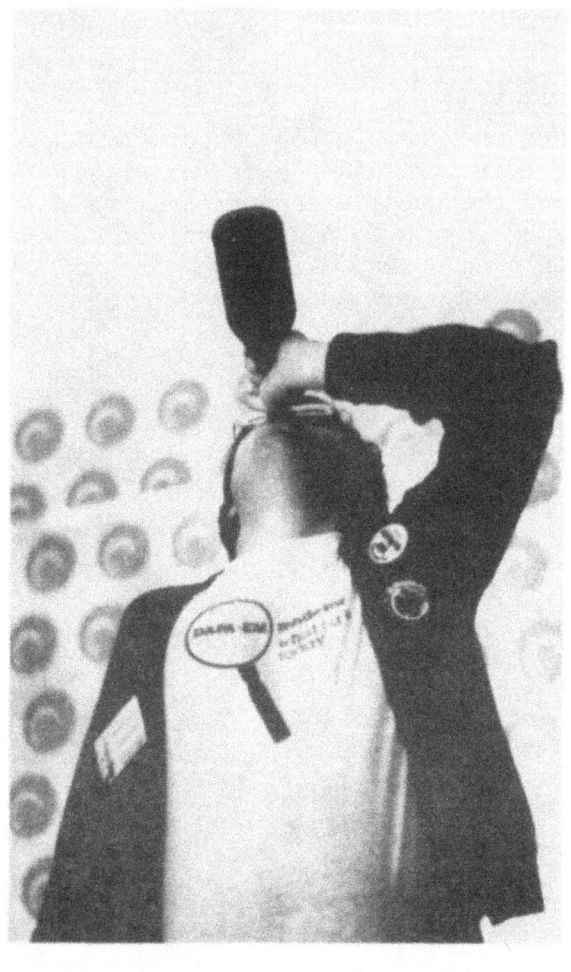 Most of the photos in the pages that follow are John's, although some, such as the one at the right, here--of Martin Wooster in a pose with which we all became familiar as the weekend wore on-- were taken by me, or at least with my camera (there were a few shots on my film that I *know* I didn't take).

Nieminski has graced this issue with a report of the official Bouchercon goings-on, and some of you who were not there may easily have gotten the idea that we spent all our time sitting around listening to speeches and panel discussions. Nothing could be further from the truth.

Sure, the programs, arranged by co-conspirators Jon Lellenburg and Peter Blau [*shown flanking Chris*
Steinbrunner in the photo below, with a shadowy Bill Crider just visible at the right] were interesting, and the guest of honor [*Gregory McDonald, shown above speaking to Ed Hoch, center, and Guy Townsend and Bubbles Grochowski at the left of the photo*] was well-

chosen, but the pleasure of informal chats with the pros who were in attendance [*such as Ed Hoch, right, who is as affable in person as he is prolific in print*] and with other fans was and always will be the greatest attraction of Bouchercons.

Some fans [*such as Bubbles Grochowski, who will be hosting the Milwaukee Bouchercon next year, Bill Crider, a Texan who has the temerity to think that he looks more like Archie Goodwin than I do, and Marv Lachman, of It's About Crime fame, all shown in the photo below*]

came early and started socializing before Bouchercon officially opened, while others didn't get in until Friday night or even Saturday morning. [*It was, in fact, on Saturday morning that the above photo of Hal Rice, Art Scott, Bob Briney, and Steve Stilwell was snapped as they returned from breakfast. The fellow at the extreme left of the above photo is a Robert Redford look-alike who was not in any way connected with Bouchercon. The chap in the photo at left is the irrepressible Bob Fish, who always brightens the Bouchercons he attends--which is most of them.*]

The great thing about a Bouchercon is the way it brings folks together. [*For example, Bill Crider and Ellen Nehr have known each other for years through DAPA-EM, but Bouchercon was the first time they had met face to face; you can see from the photo at the right how close they managed to become in a very short time.*]

Of course, not all of the people at Bouchercons see eye to eye on every thing. [*The photo below shows everybody's friend, Bob Briney, towering over Steve Stilwell and Kathi Maio. Don't let the smiles fool you; shortly after this photo was snapped Stilwell*

revealed himself to feminist Maio as an unrepentant male-chauvanist porker while I stood innocently by and watched.] But the gatherings were generally congenial. *[The photos on this page are fairly typical. In the above picture Mrs. and Mr. Bill Crider and John Nieminski are shown waiting helplessly to get a word in as Ellen speaks. At the left, Walter Albert scratches his mustache as Jim McCahery and Jeff Meyerson listen to someone (probably Ellen, as usual) expound volubly on some subject or another.]*

Usually, fans meeting for the first time were instantly at ease with each other. [*When, captured forever in the photo at right, language professors Don Yates and Walter Albert first met, they immediately fell to talking in French. I was sitting in front*  *of them and can, therefore, quote part of what was said. Don's first words were, "There is a cat in the house of my aunt," to which Walter brightly responded, "Waiter, where is the bathroom, if you please?" Below, Ellen holds forth to a stunned Art Scott and a bewildered Hal Rice. The fourth person in the photograph, at the extreme right, is Walter Albert, who, if the expression on his face is any indication, did not get a satisfactory answer to his above quoted question.*]

Many big-name fans showed up for this year's Bouchercon. [*Including, in the photo at the right, Jeff Meyerson, publisher of the fanzine,* **The Poisoned Pen,** *and, in the photo below, Walter Albert, a regular contributor to most fanzines in the mystery field (who ate that flower in one bite an instant after this shot was taken), and Art Scott, official editor of DAPA-EM, the mystery amateur publication association, who recently expelled me from that organization because I fell a couple of pages behind. (Anyone wishing to join me in sending hate mail to Art should feel free*

to do so.]

The real fun of Bouchercons is found in the room parties. [*And the official host of all the best unofficial Bouchercon parties is the fellow at the right, Hal Rice. If there were no Hal Rice, we would just have to invent one. Hal generously-- some would say foolheartedly--*

surrenders his room for parties at all Bouchercons, cheerfully and fearlessly running the risk of waking up the next morning with a Martin Wooster under his bed. In the photo below, Marv Lachman boozes it up while Hank Davis extolls the virtues of Diana Rigg to Jim McCahery. Jim Goodrich, extreme right, casts a wary eye on the recumbent form of Martin Wooster, out of sight on the floor below.]

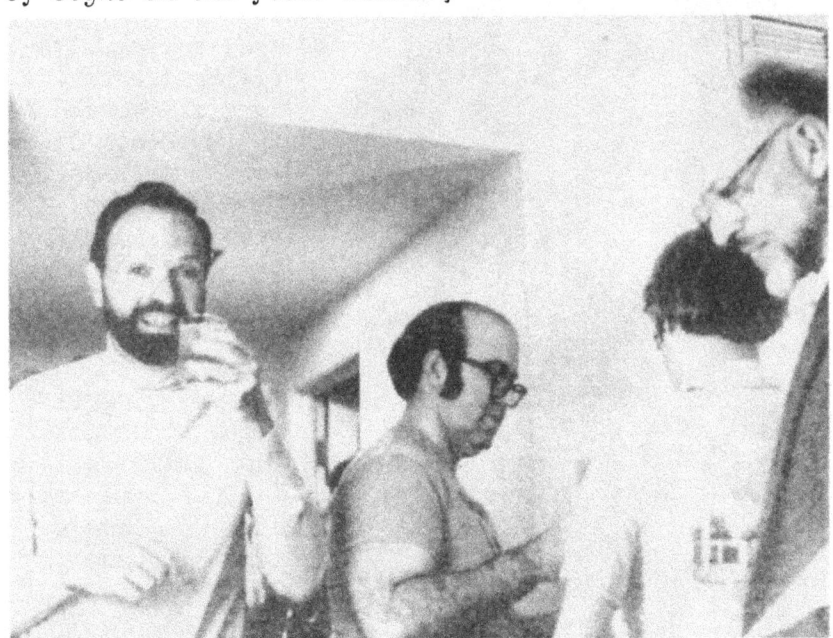

These parties are well-attended, and sitting space is usually at a premium. [Above, English fan and writer Bob Adey is reduced to sitting on the floor to sign Ellen Nehr's copy of Twentieth Century Crime and

Mystery Writers. Seated on the bed are Jeff Meyerson, Judy Koutek, Leslie Schaechter, & Jackie Meyerson. In the photo at left, Art Scott gets ready to snap another of the 1,436 photos he took at this year's gathering. In the background I stand observantly by as Kathi Maio prepares to deliver a karate chop to Steve's neck. (Steve is out of sight.)

Every party is filled with wit and sparkling dialogue. [*This year the honor of Most Sparkling was shared by Marvin Shibuk (shown at right delivering the punchline of one of his Debbie Reynolds jokes) and Martin Wooster. Their snappy repartee had party-goers rolling in the aisles alongside Martin himself, who was already there for other reasons.*

   Below, Steve Stilwell, Art Scott, and Ellen Nehr chortle as good old Marvin Shibuk blows smoke out of his ears. (Unfortunately, Marvin is not shown here.)]

Regrettably, a considerable amount of demon rum does get consumed at these gatherings. [*In the photo at right, John Nieminski laughs uproariously at Marvin Shibuk's antics, moments before tumbling unconscious from his precarious perch (bottom photo). Fortunately, John was not hurt, his fall having been broken by Dorothy Nathan, who was seated directly in front of him at the time. Ellen Nehr, shown talking (as usual) at lower right, took John's spill in stride; she simply repeated the few words which had been drowned out by the thump and went on (and on,...).*

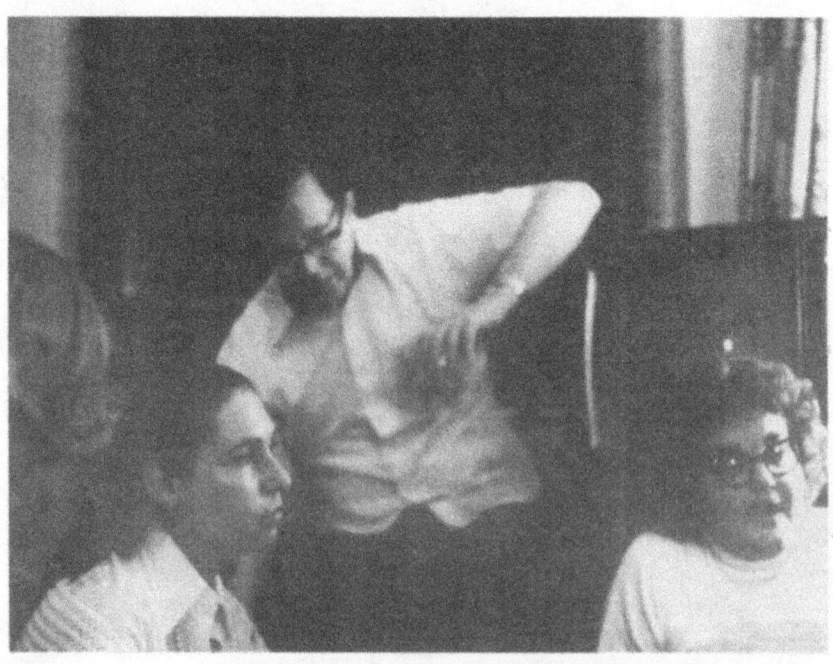

It's About Crime

By Marvin Lachman

Lachman's Second Law (the first is "Never Assume Anything") states: "Never Read a Novel with a Swastika on the Cover; They're All bad." After reading the first few chapters of Sean Flannery's *Eagles Fly* (Charter, 1980, $2.75), I thought I had found the exception to the rule. It started promisingly, albeit a bit too much like Levin's *The Boys from Brazil*. Then, things went precipitous precipitously as the Nazi S.S. Alumni Association implement their 35-year-delayed plan for world domination. They arrange to have a hypnotized look-alike take over as Vice President of the United States. The next step is to assassinate the President. Only a plastic surgeon, duped into doing the operation on the false "Veep", stands in their way. If all this is to your taste, you'll find *Eagles Fly* a fast-moving, readable book.

There are no Styles Court Irregulars, and banquets do not regularly honor Poirot and Hastings, but books about Agatha Christie are still coming off the literary assembly line. *The Agatha Christie Companion* by Russell H. Fitzgibbon (Bowling Green University Popular Press, hardcover $15.95, paperback $8.95) breaks no new ground but is useful. A third of the book's 178 pages is an alphabetical list of the characters in the Christie Canon. There is also a guide to all of Christie's series characters, including some with whom we are not so familiar. Finally, there is a capsule history of detective fiction and brief essays on Christie and her detectives. A nice introduction, for someone about to be "hooked" on Christie.

Randall Toye's *The Agatha Christie Who's Who* (Holt, Reinhart and Winston, $12.95) explores similar ground, but in greater depth, since it has well-written paragraphs about more than two thousand characters who appear in her work. There is also a very brief bibliography and even a cross-word puzzle inserted. Drawings by Ron Berg add to the book's attractiveness, but the best illustration of all is a fine cover painting of Christie by Tom Adams.

There are several reasons why Robert Barnard's *A Talent to Deceive* (Dodd, Mead, $10) is unusually interesting. Subtitling his book "an appreciation," Barnard, nonetheless, spends a portion of his 125 page essay playing devil's advocate and describing such Christie weaknesses as her snobbishness and indifferent writing. Then, lest we think this book was intended to be called "a depreciation," Barnard, a popular mystery writer himself, does a fine job of capturing her appeal (and that of the traditional whodunit). His analysis of a neglected Christie classic, *Murder in Retrospect*, is perfect.

Barnard has his faults. He repeats the myth about Christie's unwillingness to give interviews. She may have been reluctant, but she was interviewed fairly often in England and even in this country on her trip here in 1966. He also ignores inflation, stating that $50 per day is the going rate for Private Eyes. That fee hasn't been Private Operative for at least a decade. One hundred dollars a day is a bargain; Walter Wager has a detective who charged $400 a day last year.

Dorothy Sayers is frequently criticized; Barnard is not able to catch the appeal of *Gaudy Night*. He's more perceptive regarding Ngaio March, pinpointing her one major weakness, the lengthy interviews which do not advance her plots.

The bibliography by Louise Barnard is unnecessarily lengthy, containing more dates regarding the frequent reprinting of Christie books than we either need or want. Incidentally, the handling of her alternate titles (changed when they appeared in this country) could not be much more awkward. Often, both titles are repeated on succeeding pages, as if the reader's attention span is too small to remember from page 42 to page 44 that *What Mrs. McGillicuddy Saw* was originally called *The 4.50 from Paddington* in England. I'm still waiting for a Christie book which will give the original date of publication and the location of her short stories *before* they were collected in book form. *That* would be a bibliography!

Still, with no new Christie for Christmas, reading about her is the next best thing. Mr. Barnard has written the longest and best essay on Christie that I've read so far.

I've spent more time with Kevin B. Hancer's *The Paperback Price Guide* (Harmony Books, $9.95) than I have with almost any other book. While I am opposed in principle to the idea of a guide to set what we will pay for our paperback fix, I am selfish enough to have my internal cash register ringing as I compare my collection to Hancer's prices. The book is remarkably error-free, with virtually no typos and few omissions.

It is hard to judge the fairness and accuracy of Hancer's prices. Many seem high, but most are not too far out of line with those I've seen on some recent book lists and in mystery book stores. My biggest quarrel is over his prices on books with Robert McGinnis covers. Generally, the books he lists were published between 1939 and 1959. McGinnis's heyday began in the 1960's. Still, there are McGinnis covers among the books listed, e.g., the Dell D300 series, and the prices quoted are ridiculously low: 50¢ in good condition. Let us hope that between now and a second edition Mr. Hancer will learn how highly regarded McGinnis covers are and price them accordingly. This will permit many of us to realize a profit some day for the books we have, up to now, merely been slavering over.

There is one bonus in this book worth mentioning: cover illustrations from hundreds of books. Most are in black and white, but 72 are in color, albeit not as large as one would hope for. Still, they give a pretty idea of the art work that makes collecting paperbacks so much fun.

The Bibliography of Crime Fiction is full of intriguing titles that I will never get to read. I'd probably be better off, too, since most of them are not very good. Still, when books like the duo I will discuss below appear inexpensively in places like Salvation Army Stores, they are irresistible. If they're also a bit of fun to read, that is a bonus.

Harrington Strong's *Who Killed William Drew* (1925) is not very subtle, but it contains some surprises and moves quickly. Its hero, Detective Bleek, is one of those policemen of the twenties who devote all their waking hours to the job. Police unions have changed all that.

George Goodchild's *Jack O'Lantern* (1929) is an example of the master-criminal era. Fighting the titular villain is Inspector Wrench who is put under considerable pressure because "Scotland Yard has to justify its existence." It's a fast-moving book which, like Strong's, contains surprises.

I enjoyed both (who wouldn't with detectives named Bleek and Wrench), but I didn't believe a word of either.

Also fun is Ron Goulart's *Skyrocket Steele* (Pocket Books, $2.25), a mix of science fiction, espionage, and nostalgia. Set in Hollywood in 1941, it is a spoof on serials, pulp magazines, and interplanetary invaders. Goulart has been known to mention real mystery fans in his books. Is it coincidence that here he includes "Fritz Penzler and his Silver Shirts-- the German-American Horseman League"?

In past columns I've recommended mysteries for youngsters. One that would be pretty good for teenagers is Susan Dodson's *The Creep* (reprinted by Archway Books, a division of Pocket Books, Inc., $1.95). The narrator, Sabrina, agrees to act as decoy under police protection to trap a rapist who has been roaming her suburban Pittsburgh neighborhood. She's a likeable kid, and the dialogue and the situation is quite an improvement over Nancy Drew in that here is a crime that matters.

It's probably not cricket to review a book that one has co-written and co-edited, but the legendary *Detectionary* has just been reprinted by Ballantine for $2.95. Otto Penzler, Chris Steinbrunner, Charlie Shibuk, Mike Nevins, and I wrote it in 1971 on commission from Hammermill-Bond which wanted to push their reference book paper. The first edition was not distributed because, while entirely readable, there were minor imperfections in the paper. Virtually all copies were destroyed by a flood in June 1972. Existing copies are very rare and valuable. Hammermill bond did a second edition in 1972, and Viking's Overlook Press did a hardcover in 1977 and a trade paperback in 1979. Now, here comes Ballantine with a "popular" paperback edition.

Detectionary consists of hundreds of brief biographical sketches of fictional detectives (and their assistants) and villains. There are also descriptions of many of the books, short stories, and movies in which they appear. It was fun to write and fun to read. I may be prejudiced.

[*With this column Marv sent a note which read in part: "One correction. In my last column, I typed the word 'metaphoritis'--a word I coined to denote the inflated use of metaphors, as by Ross Macdonald. You printed it as 'metamoritis'-- which isn't in the dictionary either."*]

Verdicts
(More Reviews)

Dana Chambers. *Some Day I'll Kill You*. Dial Press, 1939.

Dana Chambers, according to Hubin's Bibliography, wrote 12 books, seven of which feature Jim Steele, writer of half-hour thriller radio scripts and erstwhile solver of murder mysteries. This, the first of the Steele books, is set in Connecticut and Vermont, and has Steele helping his old flame, Lisa Ridgman, now married to a doctor, cope with blackmail and murder.

Written in a terse, first-person narrative, this medium hard-boiled novel is a good read. Steele is a character of interest--he drinks Scotch, smokes Chesterfields, uses Barbasol shaving cream, had a pilot's license and went to Spain to do some flying for the Loyalists--and he isn't above shooting or strangling a bad guy, as the need arises. Not that Steele is always on the delivering end--across these 288 pages Steele has his head tapped, gets tied up, is shot at with a rifle, slugged on the jaw, and kicked in the groin.

There is a delightful reference to Sherlock Holmes (the curious incident of the dog), and at one point Lisa calls Steele "Dupin". When Steele stops at a hotel on the run from some baddies, he registers as "Flash Gordon from New York."

The solution here involves a classic use of red herring. Chambers clues two possible endings right up to the very last pages, and then manages to give us a second surprise ending about the relationship between Lisa and Steele.

The only bad thing one can say about Steele is that he doesn't like swing music in any form (isn't this a sacrilege for a book written in 1939?), but one can agree with his disliking for lawyers, finding them to be parasites.

According to Hubin, Chambers was the pseudonym of Albert Leffingwell (1895-1946). My copy of *Some Day I'll Kill You*, however, has the following inscription on the front fly leaf: "To Meta Antisdel, Bon Voyage and ever so many thanks from that old Armenian traymaker, The Author, Amityville, L.I., 27 VI 39." If Chambers was in fact of Armenian descent, as indeed this inscription would seem to indicate, one doubts whether his true name was Leffingwell. Can anyone provide further information? Meta Antisdel, where are you? (Robert Samoian)

C. P. Snow. *The Affair*. Scribner's, 1960.

The late C.P. Snow will go down in literary history as a mainstream novelist rather than a mystery writer, but he made some notable contributions to crime and detective fiction. His first novel, *Death Under Sail* (1932), was a full-fledged Golden Age detective novel and an excellent one, and his last, *A Coat of Varnish* (1979), was nominated for an Edgar. Among his later novels, *The Malcontents* (1972), an account of student dissidents, is not a detective story but does have a strong whodunit element for most of its length. The eleven novels in the *Strangers and Brothers* sequence, Snow's fictional magnum opus, are not detective stories, but many of them draw on the elements and techniques of detective fiction. The central event of *The Sleep of Reason* (1968), for example, is a murder trial. *The Masters* (1951) involves no crime, but the suspense about which of the fellows of narrator Lewis Eliot's Cambridge college will be elected Master serves the same function as the whodunit element of a mystery. Trials and legal questions occur in others of the series. And one novel from the sequence, *The Affair*, has a strong enough mystery and detective angle to merit borderline inclusion in the genre.

Lewis Eliot, no longer a fellow of the college featured in *The Masters* but still a frequent visitor, becomes drawn into a controversy. A young fellow has been dismissed by the college for alleged falsification of scientific evidence, and his wife is trying to get the case reopened. The expelled scientist has finally admitted fraud existed, but claims the fraud was perpetrated by a senior associate, a respected scientist now dead. When the appearance of new evidence--some notebooks of the older scientist that suggest the possible truth of his complicity--some of the fellows, including Martin Eliot, Lewis' brother, attempt to have the question reconsidered at apparent risk of their positions in the jockeying for academic power, made more urgent by the imminent vacancy of the Master's office. The obnoxious personality of the accused scientist throws the moral issues involved into sharper relief.

Throughout the novel, along with the depiction of academic profiles that Snow did so well, the basic detective story question remains: which was guilty of the fraud, the honored elderly researcher or his ambitious young associate? And if it was the elder who was guilty, what could his motive have been? On rereading, however, I found *The Affair* less a detective story than I remembered. The discussion of the problem is apt to be more interpersonal and political than analytical in the detective story sense. The college politics are far more interesting to Snow than the detective problem. Trollope's *The Eustace Diamonds* is frequently cited as a novel with mystery novel elements but not a mystery novel treatment of those elements. The same could be said of *The Affair*. (And Trollope, of course, is considered to be Snow's principal literary model.)

I would list C.P. Snow as one of my favorite novelists, but he is decidedly not every reader's glass of port. I can imagine many readers becoming justifiably impatient with the periodic weather reports, the magesterial character analysis, the stately proceeding from one meeting or hearing or dinner party to another. But Snow really understands his people and their inter-relationships, and I have the feeling that his dons, with more gossip than literary references dropping from their lips, talk and act more like real academics than, say,

Dorothy L. Sayers' or Michael Innes' dons. His pleasantly low-key and thoughtful writing style is echoed in crime writers as various as William Haggard, Sara Woods, and Jessica Mann, though I'm not sure if these writers have been directly influenced by Snow stylistically or simply spring from a common tradition.

In the latter chapters of *The Affair*, once the hearing before the Court of Seniors is underway with Lewis Eliot acting as representative for the dismissed scientist Howard (who is not present at the quasi-judicial proceedings), the detective story feeling becomes more concentrated. There is not just the question of who faked the scientific evidence (Howard or his mentor Palairet) but also of what happened to a photograph missing from the older scientist's notebook, one that might have proved or disproved the fraud. Did someone in the college remove it because it seemed to support the opposite side of the controversy? Eliot's old enemy Nightingale is the main suspect.

One trick of mainstream writers who take on some of the accoutrements of the mystery form is to leave the question unanswered at the end, which can sometimes be appropriate in a novel but is rarely satisfactory in a mystery novel. I misremembered from my first reading of this novel that Snow did not do that, that he offered a firm solution to the mystery, if through discovery rather than detection. But on rereading I found that not to be so--the reader has a pretty good opinion as to what the truth is, but he does not know for sure, any more than does the college's Court of Seniors. But did we require an answer? In the long run, was the book really *about* whether it was Howard of Palairet who faked the evidence? No, it was about academic politics and personal standards of ethics and justice. But perhaps we ought at least to have known whether Nightingale destroyed the photograph--on that, too, Snow chooses to keep us in the dark.

I would recommend this novel to other readers without hesitation, for its plot, its people, and the issues it takes on. But I would not recommend that they go in expecting a detective story, something Snow delivers elsewhere but not here. (Jon L. Breen)

Basil Copper. *The Big Chill*. London: Robert Hale, 1972.

Basil Copper is known to American readers for his horror short stories, his Victorian-style mystery novels, and his continuation of August Derleth's Solar Pons saga. But most of his books concern the exploits of Los Angeles private eye Mike Faraday, and this series had never been published in the United States. Having often wondered what the Faraday books were like, I tried one on a recent trip to Britain. Now I know.

The tale begins rather promisingly with Faraday chucking a big man's corpse over a cliff into the Pacific. We soon learn that the big man is the missing mayor of Los Angeles, whose body has been planted in Faraday's car. The resultant investigation involves movie stars, civic corruption, and (in a segment reminiscent of Copper's gothic fiction) an action scene on the premises of an Arms and Armour Club. After Faraday's battle with an armor-wearing assassin, however, the novel goes downhill fast, and the book is ultimately as threadbare in the field of hardboiled pastiche as the author's *Curse of the Fleers* was in Holmes-era sleuthery. The book has an additional disadvantage in that it exists in a locational vacuum. Any sense of Southern California geography, speech, or general milieu is totally lacking.

Apparently Copper's mock American is good enough to satisfy the British market, but it is too far off key to convince a Stateside reader. Consider the following speech attributed to a cowboy star: "I've just let my wife know you'll be along. ... We've been under seige all today by the press and television over this terrible business about Dwight." (p. 64) There is nothing specific to object to there, but it just isn't American dialogue. It's British.

Elsewhere there are more glaring gaffes. Faraday describes an L.A.P.D. car as a "dark saloon." He refers to a brownstone apartment and urban slums--these are American references, but not L.A. references. I don't think an American would refer to the mayor as "His Worship" even facetiously, as Faraday's girl Friday does. People are constantly eating kidneys for breakfast. Faraday refers to a "coloured" woman, possible but not probably from a seventies American of any sensitivity. Faraday drinks an "iced beer" (redundant). The British phrases "on holiday" and "to be going on with" occur, as does a reference to a car's bonnet. Finally, I don't think an L.A. private eye would make the assumption about the inferiority of California wines implicit in the following: "I got outside a steak dinner and half a bottle of white wine. The wine hadn't been made in California either. It might actually have come from Europe." (p. 38)

Solecisms aside, the style is cliché-ridden. Copper takes on the superficial conventions of the hardboiled school without adding anything of his own. Repeated references to Faraday's trench-coat and the incredibly long legs of the female lead don't help any. Figures of speech seem rather strained. "The big man was heavier than a lapsed nun's conscience." (p.10)

I think Carter Brown is the only author to prove successful in the U.S. market doing phony American backgrounds. James Hadley Chase, for example, never really caught on here. As long as the firm of Robert Hale can't get enough American detection to satisfy their clientele, there will be a place for Mike Faraday and his brethren, but I doubt they'll be crossing the water very soon. (Jon L. Breen)

Oliver Banks. *The Rembrandt Panel*. Little, Brown, 1980, 268 pp., $11.95.

Subtitled "A Novel" on the dustjacket, this book is fundamentally a love story/art history lesson rolled into one. But because of the crimes of murder and art theft (a stolen panel suspected of being a genuine Rembrandt), it also qualifies as a mystery.

From the very first chapter the author's informative writing piques your interest. The ins and outs of detecting original art versus copies, the "cadillacs and volkswagons" of art galleries, the casual name dropping of Old World Masters; all serve to entertain as well as weave a unique atmosphere about the matter at hand. Amos Hatcher, private investigator working for the IAAD (International Association of Art Dealers), decides to join forces with two Boston policemen, Captain O'Rourke and Lieutenant Callahan, to solve two murders linked by a missing baroque painting. More puzzling still, these events are without apparent motive, much the same as the case of the stolen Greek vase Hatcher left behind unconcluded in Europe. Soon involved in the plot and providing romantic interest is Sheila Woods, a knowledgeable and level-headed assistant to one of the victims.

There is some extraneous material here. Certain sections of the book seem to relegate mystery to the background, using it as a vehicle for discussion on historical and influential schools of art. This aspect will fascinate some and perhaps tire others, but Mr. Banks doesn't detour far enough to make an issue of it. Whether the reader is a connoisseur of Flemish and Dutch art or only recognizes a smattering of the information given is irrelevant. There is plenty to enjoy in just following Hatcher as he uses an unusual approach of art detection to discover the murderer and literally fill in the picture.

The Rembrandt Panel represents a first venture into the field of fiction for Mr. Banks. An earlier title, *Watteau and the North*, is a Fine Arts dissertation published in 1977. Prospects for future investigations by Amos Hatcher are limitless and intriguing--may more follow. (Becky A. Reineke)

James M. Reasoner. *Texas Wind*. Manor, 1980, 201 pp.

Readers of *Mike Shayne's Mystery Magazine* are likely to be familiar with the name of James M. Reasoner, whose stories have appeared there with regularity. The best of those stories, I think, have been the ones about a private eye named Markham. Reasoner knows what the private eye should be--tough, sympathetic, a little sentimental, and devoted to finding out the truth no matter what. So it's a pleasure to see that his first novel deals with a p.i. involved in a classic situation, the kidnapping of a rich man's daughter. The detective's name is Cody, and he's based in Ft. Worth, Texas. (The local color is really not very important to the book, but Manor has packaged it to sell to *Dallas* and *Urban Cowboy* fans, looking for more Texas chic. The cover is attractive, but a little misleading.) As in any typical case, things look much simpler than they really are; nearly everyone seems to be telling Cody the truth, but nearly everyone is lying to him. Bit by Bit he begins to piece things together, surviving in the process a truly brutal beating, and eventually finds out the things he needs to know. Reasoner writes smoothly and cleanly, with the right touch of toughness and humor. He even gives clues and plays fair with the reader. It's a tribute to his skill that though I spotted the major clue immediately, I got so caught up in events that I forgot it until he reminded me in the end. If you can't find Manor Books in your town, ask for it, or order it. James Reasoner is going to be a "name" one of these days, and his first novel is well worth looking for. (Bill Crider)

Charlotte MacLeod. *The Withdrawing Room*. Doubleday, 1980.

In Charlotte MacLeod's pleasant new novel, *The Withdrawing*

Room, she reintroduces Sarah Kelling, the young amateur detective who first appeared in *The Family Vault*. Again, Sarah manages to be both spunky and appealing, and MacLeod performs even more self-confidently in her special Kelling-novel tone, a satisfying blend of humor, charm, setting, and characterization.

Widowed and impoverished in *The Family Vault*, Sarah is now busy coping with mourning and her new career as owner of the elegant, marginally profitable boarding house into which she has transformed the kelling family brownstone on Beacon Hill. Working with a small and eccentric staff, she acquires a small and eccentric crew of boarders (One of whom is the faithful, protective Max Bittersohn), and two delightful new friends. Mary Smith is a seemingly derelict street scavenger by day and a poor-but-gracious pensioner by night. Mrs. Theonia Sorpende, one of the boarders, is a gypsy tea-leaf-reader by day and a poor-but-exotic lady by night. The money, eccentricity, and transformation motifs carry over into the murder puzzle, and thus also serve as unifying devices.

There are two murders, and the victims are the consecutive occupants of Sarah's former drawing room, now the prime suite in the boarding house. The first is a genuine eccentric, grouchy, trouble-making Mr. Quiffen. The second is the equally odd but pleasantly boring Mr. Hartler. They are Sarah's early mistakes as a business-woman, but they teach her a good lesson, and she handles Mr. Hartler's irritating sister, who plans to move in and impose her wishes on the staff, with firmness and strength.

This character growth is a gratifying feature of the novel as are Sarah's genuinely brave efforts to fend off grief over the loss of her husband. This latter emotion is neatly balanced by hints of a developing romance with Max Bittersohn.

The Withdrawing Room won't be everyone's cup of tea, Mrs. Sorpende notwithstanding. Readers seeking fact action and overt violence won't like this novel, but for the many fans of the country house tale, it will be a very satisfying read. (Jane S. Bakerman)

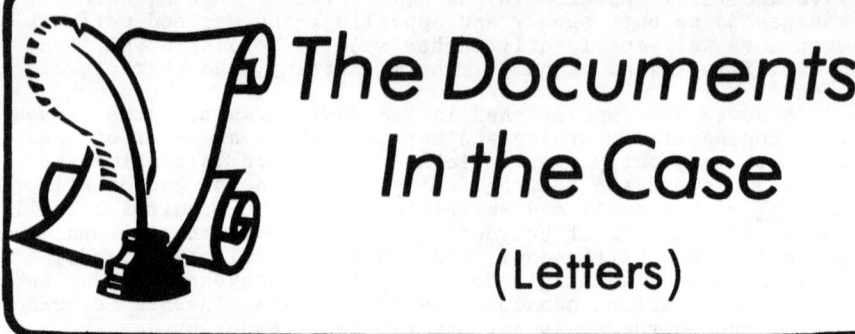

The Documents In the Case
(Letters)

From John Nieminski, 2948 Western, Park Forest, IL 60466:
   I'd hate like hell to pick up the next installment of USPS Publication No. 428-590 and find myself staring at the obituary issue of mystery fandom's second best fanzine, and so I hasten to respond affirmatively to your call for a show of hands on the question of an increase in the subscription fee. Two bucks a throw really doesn't seem out of line in this day and age of stapleless ten-bit paperbacks, not to mention glossy $4 fanzines with non-existent subscription departments. If you promise not to abscond to Brazil with the proceeds, you can count me in. And if it will help to ease the cost burden, why not just forget the promised payment for both this letter and the Bouchercon write-up? Frankly, I've always felt guilty about accepting your checks, especially since you get so much better stuff from people like Steve Lewis and Marv Lachman for practically nothing. But please don't tell my agent, who still hasn't forgiven me for ghosting "The Nero Wolfe Saga" gratis.
   I found the September/October number up to TMF's usual standard from first to last, which is to say crammed with entertaining and informative grist, disfigured by no more than your standard quota of typos. As a hard-core Sherlockian who has not yet had his fill of commentary about the Great Man, I was not at all unhappy with your decision to give pride of place this time around to Bleiler's review of *The Published Apocrypha*. I would guess than even non-Holmesians found his assessment interesting thanks to his adroit mixture of description and speculation, and it was nice to see such a specialized book get such extended treatment at the hands of a reliable critic. Since his facts are otherwise accurate, I assume that the TMF typist is responsible for the erroneous references to "Dr. Roylott". In the stage version of "The Speckled Band", which Bleiler discusses, the not-so-good doctor was re-named "Rylott", for reasons probably not even Doyle could have explained. [*John, you certainly do bring out the worst in me-- I have a well-nigh uncontrollable urge to stick out my tongue and shout YAAAA as I type the following words: it was Roylott in the MS I received from Ev.*]
   And you won't get any complaints from me about this Drood kick you seem to be on either. It's been years since I last read the Dickens novel and I have only the sketchiest familiarity with the literature, but I gobble up everything about the subject that comes along and did so also with the Ben Pot-

ter piece. Droodians may not be as numerous as their Sherlockian counterparts, but you always know when they're around; their fervor is almost as infectious and it's always fun to watch the fur fly when competing theorists have a go at one another. I have yet to finish a Droodian exegesis without coming away firmly convinced that here at last is the correct solution to *The Mystery*, no matter how far-fetched the thesis. If I had to choose sides in the who-is-Dick-Datchery controversy, I'd probably go along with those who argue that it was Helen hiding under that wig. Most people find the notion too hard to swallow, but then they never saw my high school class: we had several girls who looked like old men when they dressed up....

Marv Lachman's column isn't at all long enough to satisfy me and you sumply must try to get him to offer up larger helpings of his own special brand of informed commentary, even if it means that we'll have to suffer more of those outrageous puns which he suddenly seems to have developed a penchant for. I see by this installment that he too thinks that Helen MacInnes gets away with overly padded plots; and it's nice to know that we share the same favorable opinion of the Encyclopedia Brown books, which I used to peek into now and then when my kids weren't looking. But I must say that I don't know what to make of his seeming inability to name more than three Jewish detective characters in the mystery fiction field. I know for a fact that he thinks highly of James Yaffe's "Mom", who fits the definition even though she falls in the amateur category. And I can't believe that he has not yet encountered in his travels either Meyer Meyer of Ed McBain's 87th Precinct or the Lockridges' Lt. Nathan Shapiro. Sol Weinstein's Oy-Oy-7 may not be a detective exactly, but he's certainly in the genre, and what about Henry Klinger's Lt. Shomri Shomar of the Tel Aviv Police Department? I'll be surprised if your readers can't come up with other nominees, and unless I hear otherwise I'm going to assume Marv is guilty of a little leg-pulling intended to generate a response or two, a ploy you yourself are not unfamiliar with, you devil. [*John, John, what flights of fantasy you are capable of.*]

Mike Clancy's "Saint's preserve us!" was a short-lived catch phrase in my circles back in the early 1940s, a memory kindled by Carl Larsen's piece on the delights of the old "Mr. Keen" radio program. The lead actor that I remember best was not Bennett Kilpack, who doesn't ring a bell at all, but Arthur Hughes, who sounded to me at the time like a slightly sterner version of "Just Plain Bill", another old favorite in those days. Somewhere along the line the show wound up in competition with some comedy offering, a development which cut me off abruptly from contact with Clancy, much to my regret. "Easy Aces", I think it was, whose Jane Ace drove me up the wall with her vocal whine, and whose own special delightfulness I didn't come to appreciate until much later. Larsen's suggestion that the Keen character "had no previous existence in books" is subject to challenge, depending on how precisely he defines his operative words. Back in 1906, Appleton published a collection of five stories authored by Robert Chambers entitled *The Tracer of Lost Persons*, which featured one Westrel Keen, whom Ellery Queen later characterized as a "love detective". Chambers' Keen reportedly differs in important respects from his aural successor, but there are those who believe that

the one inspired the other, including Randy Cox, who not only
reviewed the book at some length in the July 1971 issue of TAD,
but who also reminisced therein about the radio program in
much the same vein as Larsen.

Barry Van Tilburg's spy series dossiers are little treasure troves of useful information about the characters who populate that sub-genre, and a handy guide to the contents of the discouragingly large number of books yet to see publication on this side of the Atlantic. Like David Doerrer, I hope this feature has a long run. The compiler somehow neglected to list Bulldog Drummond's given name (Hugh) and Mr. Moto's initials (I.O.) in the latest installment, which probably won't earn him any demerits, but someone like Charlie Shibuk is almost sure to call him on his assertion that George Sanders portrayed Drummond on the screen. Unless all of my movie reference books are in error, the job wah handled on a couple of occasions not by Sanders but by his brother, Tom Conway. I caught neither of the two films he did, and as a matter of fact have seen only a handful of the rather large number that have appeared to date. Drummond is one of those book characters whom no one seems born to impersonate, like Archie Goodwin and Travis McGee. My favorite was Ronald Coleman, in some respects the least likely candidate of all.

It wasn't until I got to the last page of Jeff Banks' B-film memoir that I found listed a movie that failed to ring a responsive chord, and until that point I felt like I was reading the reminiscences of my own personal doppleganger. Like Banks, most of my own youth was frittered away in one darkened theater or another, at least on Saturdays and Sundays, and I have this feeling that between us he and I have buried in our memory cells the flickering images of just about every serial and series film ever inflicted on the impressionable adolescents of our generation, except maybe for the Bulldog Drummond epics. I was less critical of the Charlie Chan saga than he, but we otherwise seem to have had remarkably similar tastes (or the equivalent lack thereof). One audience reaction of the time that he did not see fit to mention: the derisive catcalls that resounded throughout the pleasure palaces at the unlikely modes of escape from death and destruction that some of our serial heroes resorted to. Most of them were as hard to swallow as you own modes of egress from gainful employment.... [*Just wait until you hear the latest, John.*]

From Ev Bleiler, still in hiding in New Jersey:

Thanks for the latest issue of TMF. I hope that the signs and omens do not come to pass, and that you keep TMF going. It fills a gap.

I for one will pledge--this sounds like the local public TV station--a twelve-note to keep the mag alive. Twelve bucks is a lot, but I still save money. It's cheaper to let you print my occasionals than to pay for it myself.

Have you considered alternatives? Perhaps trying to get university support locally? [*A good idea, that; if I can just settle down long enough in an area with a university close at hand.*] I know that they don't have much money, but the amount that would be involved is not great by project standards. One can economize and forego the hand-made paper with deckle edges, the five-color art work, and the hand-calligraphed headings.

[*It's nice to know than my artistic touches have not gone unnoticed.*]

I know that the U. of Cal. sponsorship of TAD proved bad, as everyone predicted, but there may be controls for such things? ("Everyone" in the previous line means me and a couple of others.)

Carl Larsen's article on Mr. Keen awakened feelings of nostalgia. I remember the program from the late 1930's, when I was a kid. Mr. Keen's smarmy voice comes back to me clearly, though I don't recall a thing about his cases.

The series, by the way, did have a literary origin. Mr. Keen(e) [*Ha--you missed that, didn't you, John?*] (without the first name of Bayard, as I recall from the radio, and somewhat differently characterized) came from the book *The Tracer of Lost Persons* by Robert W. Chambers. I believe that some of the stories in the book also saw periodical publication, though I am not sure about this.

I was delighted to see that you have at least one more Droodian among your subscribers. Ben Fisher's article made me think a little, though I do not agree with him. To mention a couple of main points: (1) The ring. Most students agree that the ring is going to play a part in the denouement of the story, though exactly what part depends on one's understanding of the story. But I do not see that Grewgious's mentioning of the ring to Bazzard means that Bazzard is Datchery. This seems to me a non sequitur. One could as well say that it indicates Grewgious as Datchery, which is impossible. My own guess is that this incident is simply Dickens' way of pointing out a clue dramatically to the reader. (2) The cover illustration. You and your readers may not have seen this, since it is not usually reproduced in trade editions of *Drood*. In its final version by Sir Luke Fildes it consists of a floral device, broken up into little cartouches and panels, within which are set little action scenes. (I don't have a copy handy here in the office and I hope that my memory is not playing me false.) How this cover is to be taken has always been problematic. No one really knows how much of it is Dickens and how much is the artist, how much is thematic, and how much is decorative. The majority opinion, with which I would go along, is that the pictorial parts of the cover probably represent events, although it is not clear how far one should push them in literalness: they may be symbolic rather than literal. As for the decorative floral element, who knows? Such panelled floral title pages were not rare in Victorian publishing and they are often just decorative. But again, I don't see that this has anything really to do with Bazzard.

My reasons for rejecting Bazzard are in my old paper, and I think they still stand. The old paper, I think in retrospect, should have stressed Datchery's emotional situation more than it did. Datchery hates Jasper, even before he meets him. This would be out of character for Bazzard, and certainly no part of his proposed role as agent of Grewgious.

Your and Claude Saxon's suggestion that Bazzard may be only a facet of Datchery is a new one on me. I would have to go back to the text to check it, though from memory it does not seem to fit.

From Charles Shibuk, 2084 Bronx Park East, Bronx, NY 10462:
Allow me to register a resounding YES to your proposal to

raise the subscription rate.

Anyone who does not resubscribe to TMF (barring dire economic necessity) is either a fool or a knave. [*That's telling 'em, Marvin!*]

The quality of life would be infinitely poorer without the existence of TMF.

The current issue contains a few errors--many of which should have been avoided by a quick check of *The Encyclopedia of Mystery and Detection*.

Jeff Banks refers to Charlie Chan "serials" several times, but there was only one: *The House Without a Key* (1926) which he has not seen.

Furthermore, no Michael Shayne film was ever based on a Biggers novel. (Try Clayton Rawson.) Nor did Ronald Colman ever essay the role of Philo Vance. (Try William Powell.)

While we're at it, Mr. Van Tilburg should be informed that many actors have played Bulldog Drummond, but George Sanders wasn't one of them. (Try his brother Tom Conway.)

If Mr. Larsen thinks that Mr. Keen had no previous existence, he might try to locate *The Tracer of Lost Persons* (Appleton, 1906) by Robert W. Chambers.

I'm surprised to see that Mike Nevins, whose bibliographical skills are immense, thinks that there are only two (rather than three) Melville Fairr novels--or is this one of those sinister editorial typos? [*I certainly would like to know how the myth that TMF is riddled with typos ever got started. Nothing, of course, could be further from the truth. In the present instance, for example, Mike's letter says two, not three.*]

I would personally relish details about your business scheme involving a duck and a peg-legged dwarf. [*Alas, Marvin, it is a tale for which the world is not yet ready ....*]

In return, I'll promise never to reveal the real (and disgustingly loathsome) reason why I was obliged to punch and forcibly eject you from the genial Hal Rice's room during the recent Bouchercon. [*On second thought, perhaps I could make an exception in your case, Marvin.*]

From Frank Floyd, Rt. 3, Box 139-F, Berryville, AR 72616:

Yes, Guy, I would pay twelve dollars for the next subscription of *The MYSTERY FANcier*; I would even pay more than this amount if it were necessary. I say so only after some pondering over the matter. By word count two dollars an issue is kind of expensive when compared to large commercial magazines. Therefore, what I am willing to pay for is the uniqueness that is peculiar to *The MYSTERY FANcier* and would be difficult if not impossible to find in another magazine. For some time I have wondered whether a day might come when you would feel that you were inadequately rewarded for your very apparent editorial talents, the demanding labor, and the long hours you must have to put in. I knew that your compensation could not be financial; however, I had never realized you were taking money out of your own pocket in order to keep *The MYSTERY FANcier* going. Guy, if you are willing to give your time and labor, the rest of us who benefit surely should be willing to do our part by coming up with the cost of publication.

There also have got to be some ways to increase the number of subscribers.

[*A later letter:*]

I can only cross my fingers that you have survived this latest move of your moves of late. I have heard of roving editors before, but *The MYSTERY FANcier* going with you each time is getting to be a roving magazine.

The letter output for the last few issues has been disappointing. I have always enjoyed the letters, but now that there are none to speak of I have come to see a greater value in "The Documents in the Case" than I had previously realized. The jokes, comments, ideas, fancies, and arguments of the letters are what add the final touches to the casual articles of *The MYSTERY FANcier* and make them personal to all of us.

In case our problem is one of having run short of topics I will try to suggest five on which I would like to hear the other readers say something via their letters.

A matter of interest to me is who everyone's favorite writers are and which stories do they like best. I would like to know each person's five favorite authors and five favorite stories. Offhand, I would say my favorite authors are Rex Stout, Edgar Allan Poe, Arthur Conan Doyle, Raymond Chandler, and Erle Stanley Gardner. I choose Stout for character and story; I choose Poe for unmatched insight; Doyle for being interesting; Chandler for style; and Gardner for writing so many readable books. As for stories, they are too many I cannot eliminate. There are several by Poe, ten or twelve by Stout, perhaps one by Doyle, something by Ross Macdonald, one by Donald Hamilton, one by any of a number of writers, something from that mass of writers who only wrote one good book but that one book was really good, and on and on.

A second thing that is probably of interest to all of us is how much sex and gore is vital to the success of a mystery story. My opinion is that most of it is not vital and sometimes none of it is. I think sex and gore, especially very raw and explicit sex and excessive gore, are a poor substitute for sense on the writer's part and reveal his immaturity. I have seen so many cars and helicopters bombed and blown up that each time I see it happen on TV I flinch in pain and am reminded of those cartoons in which the characters constantly blow each other up. I cannot build up any sympathy for, but rather feel disgust toward, those guys who slaughter fifty-five or sixty opponents in an assortment of grotesque ways in a heroic effort to recover a paste diamond or something else of equal value. I am sick of characters apparently without any real human affection whose only accomplishment in life seems to be that they have bed-hopped with every loose dairy cow, or milk factory, on three continents.

I would like to know how everyone compares TV mysteries with book mysteries. There must be some reason; I read quite a few mystery books, but I seldom watch a mystery on TV--I turn off of many, many more than I watch, anyway.

Has any of *The MYSTERY FANcier* readers ever acted in a mystery play or seen one on stage, I wonder? I never have, but a good mystery play might be really worth seeing.

Does anyone have information on who was the highest paid mystery writer of all time? If you have been counting, you know that this makes five.

Where are David Doerrer, Jeff Banks, Bill Crider, and Jane Bakerman? Where are Jon Breen, John Harwood, John Ball, and that curmudgeon Bill Loeser, alas? Where are Theodore Dukeshire, Mary Ann [*Bubbles*] Grochowski, Joe Lansdale, and Ellen

Nehr? Where are the letter writers of yesteryear? Could the cost of postage stamps be the culprit?

From Ben Fisher, Box 816, University, MS 38677:
   We must save the ship; I'll order *two* $12.00-a-year subscriptions to TMF (one for the Ole Miss Library), and I've just given your address to my friend Richard Fusco; do I get extra gold in my medal or a hood for honorary duty, or what! [*What.*] ...
   I enjoyed, as I always do, Bleiler's piece on Holmesiana. Jeff Banks' article on the B-movies, especially serials, I devoured. I may send you something on a favorite of mine: *The Crimson Ghost* (1946). That one, of course, moves into detection (who is the CG?) realms. The reviews of Reilly and the Carr collection should send fans after those two valuable books.
   Finally, having seen a similar letter recently in another zine, I'd like to comment on the negative views on "scholarly" writing, or what some persons seem to believe is that type, in zines like TMF. Having trained long and, I hope, thoroughly toward becoming a "scholar"--I am a college English professor--I have come to understand only too well the need for thoroughness in coverage of subjects like *Edwin Drood* and the literature that has grown up around it. It is really rather a bore to read articles that indicate newness in their content when what is said has been said before. That tactic is *not* the "grandest game in the world." Scholarship, or broad-deep knowledge of a subject, does not have to be deadly, as some readers apparently think it must be, no exceptions.
   For example, in combing through magazines in search of writings by Frederick Irving Anderson (I'm preparing a bibliography of his works), I've learned that he wrote not just short stories, for which he's repeatedly credited, but some longer fiction, *and* that his work is not restricted to the detective tale, although that's what many persons think. He produced at least one good supernatural tale, no surprise if we recall that Poe influenced him, and there are others that give a larger picture of him as a writer than the detective stories alone do. I'm not putting down detective fiction by any means in writing as I have here.
   P.S. I add, as a final plume for "scholarship," that those who yell the loudest against it, or what they suppose "it" is, are generally the speediest to grab up bibliographies, checklists, or whatever you call 'em, such as that mentioned above, and not only pore over them, but, typically, write letters with additions/corrections!

From Bill Loeser, P.O. Box 1702, New Bern, NC 26560:
   $12 doesn't seem too much for TMF: I declare high. Although there does seem to be a slight falling off in quality of late without the keystone of the Wolfe Saga to support the edifice. Keep trying to motivate people to write about books; the articles on movies, radio, etc. don't interest hard core readers, and it is these people who can help you get your mailing list closer to the 800 on mine. [*Fat chance.*]
   In the nature of errors and omissions, Mr. Larsen is incorrect about Mr. Keen. The series sprung from *The Tracer of Lost Persons* by Robert W. Chambers (Appleton, 1906).
   Regarding "The Line-Up", I had a note from John McAleer

some time back that he was taking over *The Thorndyke File*. His address is 121 Follen Road, Lexington, MA 02173. I also heard from Paul R. Moy, 13 Keymer Road, Brighton, East Sussex BN1 8FB, who is reviving Ethel Lindsay's *Mystery Trader* as *Crime & Detective Fiction News*. Two issues a year will be published, beginning April 1981. Subscription rates for the US are $4.00 sea mail and $6.00 air mail, conversion included. The first issue is to have a long piece on A.B. Cox (Anthony Berkeley, Francis Iles), which bodes well for its future.
 [*From a later card:*]
 Following up on my letter, I received a note yesterday from Paul R. Moy stating that *Crime & Detective Fiction News* will be a non-starter. This no doubt makes it the shortest-lived periodical in the field, expiring four months before the first issue.
 [*I, too, received a brief note from Mr. Moy, returning the check I had sent him. It read, in part: "I am writing to advise you, with profound regret, that my proposed magazine "Crime & Detective Fiction News" will not now be appearing. A Series of unforseen* [sic] *circumstances have lead me to make this heart-searching decision: ever increasing costs and unlimited time needed in replying to dozens of letters being received each week, together with business commitments which must come first." Obviously, Mr. Moy didn't know what he was getting into.*]

From Mike Nevins, 7045 Cornell, University City, MO 63130:
 Thanks for another fine TMF. Since I'm more or less on your freebie list I can't answer your big question directly, but if I were not so favored I'd certainly feel an annual subscription would be worth $12. (Especially since as a writer I can deduct the cost as a professional journal subscription!) But because of this doubly unusual status of mine, I don't think my vote should count for much. Nevertheless I hope the regular paying customers feel the same way so that you can continue to publish. [*Lest there be any confusion, I should point out that Mike's comments about being on a "freebie list" alludes to the fact that he contributes to virtually every issue and therefore pays little, if anything, for his subscription. With TMF, there's no such thing as a freebie list.*]
 No wonder Jeff Banks never saw Ronald Colman playing Philo Vance in a movie! He never did.

From Myrtis Broset, 204 S. Spalding St., Spring Valley, IL:
 I began reading the fanzine on page 3, then decided I had better read page 1 after all--perhaps you were inviting all of us to a Christmas party. Not so, you are copying the Postal Service and raising your rate. So, this leaves me thinking, "If he only gets 99 subscribers, what a loss to mystery fandom this will be. Maybe I should subscribe again, I might be the 100th one and save the fanzine."
 Have you ever read an ad for an appliance sale? They ignore the total price, everything costs just a few pennies a day. I wonder if this system will work for me. Let's see--$12.00 a year amounts to $1.00 a month. $1.00 divided by 30 is? Right! Just a few pennies a day. Gee, I feel much better already. Why didn't you think of that?
 I will enclose my check for $1.00 and next month I will send you another dollar and the month after that I——

Okay, if that's the way you feel about it, I'll pay it all at once. I could have offered to pay a few pennies every day, you know.

[*From a later letter:*]

In January, look for a book by Bill Pronzini written in collaboration with columnist Jack Anderson. Titled *The Cambodia File*, it will be published by Doubleday. It is somewhat different than Pronzini's other mystery suspense books, being based on facts gathered by Anderson. It is the story of a diplomat from the United States, stationed in Phnom Penh at the time the Khmer Rouge take over Cambodia. A book by Pronzini and Anderson! How can it miss?

Lawrence Sanders, who writes about sin and the commandments, is working on a new book titled *The Third Deadly Sin*, scheduled to be published next August by Putnam. The story is about a female mass murderer and, as in the other two books of this series, the detective is Delaney, retired from the New York City police force. If you enjoyed the first two *Sins*, you will be looking forward to the new one.

From Robert Samoian, 11308 Yearling St., Cerritos, CA 90701:

When I was about 10 years old (thirty years ago in 1950), I had a jig saw puzzle featuring *The Great Merlini*. Alas, it went the way of most childhood toys, discarded, given away, lost to me. I remember the puzzle included a small booklet written by Clayton Rawson, containing a short mystery story, the solution of which would be revealed by putting together the puzzle. I recall the completed puzzle showed Merlini wearing a Hindu-type turban, and the clue involved the reversal of the time on a clock in a photograph caused by flipping over the negative (10 o'clock becomes 2 o'clock, and vice versa). There were at least four of these mystery story/jig saw puzzle sets. I had another one featuring the detective team of Kelley Roos, Jeff and Haila Troy. Can anyone supply further information re these picture puzzle stories?

Miracles for Sale, mentioned in the Boucher biographical sketch of the Great Merlini, was the only movie based on a Merlini story. This 1939 MGM release starred Robert Young as the magician detective, but inexplicably his name in the movie was changed to "Mike Morgan", not nearly as colorful as the Great Merlini. Based loosely on *Death from a Top Hat*, others in the cast of *Miracles for Sale* were Florence Rice as Judy Barclay, Gloria Holden as Madame Rapport, Frederick Worlick as Dr. Cesar Sabbatt, Walter Kingsford as Colonel Watrous, Lee Bowman as Joe LaClaire, Cliff Clark as Inspector Homer Gavigan, and, in a bravura performance, Henry Hull as Dave Duvallo. The film was directed by Tod Browning of *Freaks* fame. It was an excellent who-dun-it, well made, on a par with the MGM "Thin Man" films of the time; it is regrettable the film did not spawn into a film series.

From Nancy Axelrod, 648 Orange St., New Haven, CT 06511:

One of the reasons that it's taken me so long to get settled in here is that I've spent hours and hours trying to recover from the ultimate disaster that can happen to a book collector--*mildew!* I made the mistake of storing my books for a couple of months in a basement that got flooded. Hundreds of books--including a few rare old mysteries featuring lady detectives--were cloaked in black, green, brown or red (!)

mildew by the time I discovered the problem. I've tried suggestions from a number of people, plus some of my own ideas (based on my background as a biologist)--I fanned the books out to dry in the sun, brushed and vacuumed off all the spores I could before bringing them indoors, and I even tried packing them in garbage bags filled with cedar chips to absorb the smell. (The standard fumigation procedures for mildewed papers are too impractical for handling books, especially this many.) Most of the spores are now gone, but water marks and mildew stains remain, and my apartment smells to high heaven! Do you have any helpful suggestions, other than to throw the books away? HELP!
   [*I can't help you, Nancy, but if there is a cure to your problem I dare say some TMFer knows about it, and these pages are available for any suggestions.*]

From Barry Van Tilburg, 4380-67th Ave. N., Pinellas Park, FL:
   Am eagerly awaiting (you probably get tired of hearing this) the next issue. I particularly liked the article about Charteris and the Saint (having read them during my grade school through high school years) and the reviews in volume 4 number 4. The Saint was always one of my favorite adventurers as a child. Growing up during the Sixties, the Saint was everywhere. Reprints of books by MacFadden-Berkeley, the television series with Roger Moore as the Saint, and of course the Saint magazine which became must reading during my free hour in high school (after homework, of course).

From Elmore Mundell, 5560 Evergreen Ave., Portage, IN 46368:
   Your printer, whoever he is, and whatever he's charging, is doing a first class job. Photographing type-written copy, and doing it well, is a tough job. Very fine.
   And your editorial policy, from an examination of just one issue, is unobtrusive, and nobody lectures me. Information is what I want, about anything related to detective stories. My own inclination is to use the strictest possible construction to "detective story."
   [*From a later letter:*]
   Just worked myself back to 3/3.
   The letter from E. Stewart--the thing she copied is part of "A Comp's-eye View of Punctuation." Walling is a retired professor of English from the University of Wisconsin, who is also a private printer--The Sumac Press of La Crosse, Wisc. He also did "A Comp's Eye View of Paper," "A Comp's Eye View of Cats" (for Catalogs), and "A Comp's Eye View of Type."
   [*From yet another letter:*]
   Count on me for the higher rate.
   But I'm not sure--I think I resent anyone's getting a free ride. I think that most of the contributors--letter writers for sure--should be thankful that they have a forum in which to sound off....
   As you say, most people have no conception of the work involved.
   I printed a checklist of detective stories. It ran 340 pages, octavo, about 5½ x 7. I printed 15 copies, and copyrighted it. And then the fun began. I received about 200 requests for copies, from some who offered to pay. Most of the requests I ignored, but a few I had to answer. And I answered saying that I couldn't and wouldn't afford to sell

for a nominal cost, but would trade for something I really wanted. Never got a trade, but was more or less forced to justify my position. And it went like this—
   (a) About $200 for type and accessories.
   (b) To set and distribute type for re-use, each page 1½ hours.
   (c) Print each page, one page at a time, ½ hour.
   (d) Fold and collate, 40 hours.
   (e) $6 each to bind.
   At slave labor costs--and I couldn't hire anybody to help--$2/hour. It took about 10 months.
   Type--$200; labor--$1440; binding--$90; total--$1730, or about $120 per book.
   I didn't sell any--I did give half a dozen away. I finally traded a set of unbound sheets for a copy of Hubin's book and some other stuff.

From Carl Larsen, 3872 Amboy Road, Staten Island, NY 10308:
   Getting the latest issue has galvanized me into writing, if only to assure you that I will continue, even at $12, to subscribe to your journal. Putting prices into perspective, that's still a tremendous bargain. I'm sure that you will get a vote of confidence from the shareholders, as well as threats to your person and property.
   TMF 4:4 was enjoyable reading, especially the trip through Drood-land. Although I've made that trip before, I felt that E.F. Bleiler had a sure hand and was almost totally convincing. His building of negative cases was much more efficient than the gathering of positive evidence with which the subject is usually encumbered. I wonder what Mr. Bleiler would do with my thought that "Grewgious" springs from "egregious" which means, of course, out of the herd. A modest suggestion for you: why not turn your attention to this matter? Drood, that is, not the herd.
   Marv Lachman was also, as usual, quite interesting. Letting these buffs ramble is something TMF does well. The play of an informed and critical mind over any field is always a joy to watch. Ellen Nehr's LOL was another interesting essay with some witty and perceptive observations. Perhaps we could match up some of the LOM with some of the LOL. Miss Marple and Asey Mayo, say? I recently bought and read (both regretted) an attempt to present one of each sex in one book. This first of a series is called *Exit Actors, Dying* and is, I think, pretty dreary. [*Ellen loved it.*] One eccentric to a book, please--unless you happen to be Charles Dickens.
   I'm going to try Merlini after reading Fred Dueren's piece. If the books live up to the biographical note, they ought to be worthwhile. As for that lengthy opus on Simon Templar and his creator, I read it with much interest, searching for typos, etc. I found myself less charitable in that area on my own words than I am towards others! In school we were often reminded of an Italian proverb to the effect that a translator is a traitor. If there is a Swedish equivalent, I hope that it is not being muttered darkly over the now-frozen North. I'd hate to find a group of Vikings swarming over my lawn waving their swords.
   Steve Lewis is still one of TMF's major strengths.

www.ingramcontent.com/pod-product-compliance
Lightning Source LLC
Chambersburg PA
CBHW031434040426
42444CB00006B/813